SAUDI ARABIA

FORCES OF MODERNIZATION

SAUDI ARABIA

FORCES OF MODERNIZATION

BOB ABDRABBOH

Amana Books

AMANA BOOKS
58 Elliot Street
Brattleboro, Vermont 05301

Printed in the United States of America

*To the memory of
my father*

TABLE OF CONTENTS

LIST OF TABLES

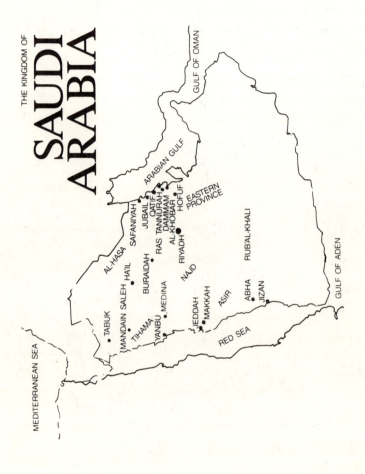

THE KINGDOM OF
SAUDI ARABIA

GULF OF OMAN

ARABIAN GULF

SAFANIYAH
JUBAIL
QATIF
RAS TANNURAH
DAMMAM
AL-KHOBAR
HOFUF
EASTERN PROVINCE

AL-HASA

HA'IL

MANDAIN SALEH

BURAIDAH

RIYADH

NAJD

RUBAL-KHALI

TABUK

TIHAMA

YANBU
MEDINA

JEDDAH
MAKKAH

ASIR

ABHA
JIZAN

GULF OF ADEN

RED SEA

MEDITERRANEAN SEA

PREFACE and ACKNOWLEDGMENT

Saudi Arabia, as a developing country, has a need for modernization in order to generate economic growth and development. This book analyzes the most significant forces responsible for the country's emergence into the modern world. Of these forces, it is Islam that is the power source that fuels Saudi Arabia. Islam serves as the framework upon which the Kingdom's political system and ideology are founded. The new force in the country is oil. However, Saudis regard Islam, not oil, as the nation's most precious resource. Thus, it is Islam that is the strongest force in the Kingdom of Saudi Arabia.

In the face of changes that the discovery of oil has brought, the Saudis are attempting to further modernize their country. It is important to emphasize that the Kingdom's aim is modernization, not Westernization.

The Saudis are trying to modernize through the use of Western technology and expertise. However, they do not want Western values or social traditions to replace the ones that have existed for centuries in Saudi Arabia. The Islamic culture will remain an important force in the modernization process and will, thus, minimize Westernization.

The major hypothesis which we will test and investigate is as follows: Until the middle of this century Saudi Arabia was one of the world's poorest countries. Today Saudi wealth and consequent political influence are derived from a) the revenue generated by oil production and, b) Islam in the Kingdom as both religion and the system of government.

The method I have used for this research is both descriptive and analytical. The study draws from literature from the Planning Ministry, the Saudi Monetary Agency, from religious leaders, personal visits and intensive interviews with many international experts on the country at the World Bank, the International Monetary Fund, and the United Nations. As a translator I have been able to obtain important information from both Arabic and English language sources.

This study attempts two tasks. The first is to explore the character of Saudi society and to contribute to an understanding of the people of Saudi Arabia, the country and its heritage. The second task is to highlight the roles of oil and Islam in the modernization of Saudi Arabia.

We will trace briefly some of the highlights of Saudi Arabia's success in the modernization process and general economic development in the post oil-boom era.

I have striven to make this study the most accurate of its kind to date, based on extensive field work over four years' time, and to achieve a balance between praise, criticism and objectivity.

I would like to thank the many people who have assisted me, too numerous to include here, for their support in making this book a reality.

Bob A. Abdrabboh, Ph. D.
January, 1985

PART ONE

INTRODUCTION

1. Geo-political Background

The Kingdom of Saudi Arabia is an independent sovereign Arab state[1]; the people are Semitic and form part of the Arab nation. Its existence as a political entity dates back to 1774. In that year, the head of the House of Saud, the present Royal Family, formed an alliance with Mohammad Ibn Abdulwahab, founder of an Islamic reform movement called "Wahhabism."

A brief examination of Wahhabism will be sufficient to inform the reader of the essence of the movement.

"It is a creed built on the oneness of the Almighty God, totally for His sake, and it is divorced from any ills or false innovation."[2]

The message of Wahhabism is straightforward; it calls for a return to classic Islam, for obedience to the pristine law, fully and strictly, and for the establishment of a society where the law dominates. Therefore, the Wahhabism interpretation of Islam is explicit, strict, and is to be seriously implemented.

---

[1]Perhaps the most extensive pre-Islamic Kingdom that existed in the Peninsula was the Nabatean civilization, which built great agricultural and trading cities. From its capital at Madain Salah, it spread into the Fertile Crescent, reaching the Dead Sea in what is now Jordan. The Nabateans were noted for advances in irrigation, water conservation and reclamation, terrace farming, and large-scale cultivation techniques.

[2]Fouad Al-Farsy, *Saudi Arabia: A Case Study in Development* (London: Stacey International, 1980), p. 33.

In 1703, Sheik Mohammad Ibn Abdulwahab was born in Najd of a highly respected and religious family, and lived to the age of 89. He called for the return to the purest form of early Islam, basing his creed on the "Sunni" Muslim school of law "Hanbali." Because of his teachings, he was forced to take refuge at Dir'iyah, the home of Al-Saud, under the protection of Prince Mohammad Ibn Saud, the ruler of Dir'iyah.[3]

At present, Dir'iyah is a small oasis town located on the Wadi Hanifa, just fifteen kilometers southeast of the capital city of Riyadh.

The story of Saudi Arabia parallels the House of Saud and its persevering efforts over several generations to create a unified state. The chronology of unification is complex and uneven; setbacks were many. But the climactic chapter begins in 1902, with the daring recapture of Riyadh[4], the traditional family seat, by the 21-year-old Abdul Aziz Ibn Saud. The next ten years were spent wresting control of the Najd from the rival Rashied family. Soon after, Ibn Saud regained Alhasa from Ottoman domination. Noteworthy here is that the daring coup which captured Riyadh is celebrated in the history of the Kingdom. But it was the night's work of May 14, 1913, which secured for the Al-Saud the most expensive real estate in the world.

The southern highlands of Asir were added to his terri-

---

[3]The growth and expansion of the town was abruptly arrested around 1819 when it was invaded and destroyed by the Egyptians, who had been incited by the Ottoman Empire.

[4]Riyadh first became the seat of the House of Saud in 1824, when it was no more than one of a string of villages along Wadi Hanafi. Today it is the Royal Capital of the Kingdom, with an estimated 1.2 million inhabitants.

tory in 1921, the Holy City of Makkah and the Hejaz were taken in 1926.[5] In 1932, Saudi Arabia was more or less united under the leadership of King Abdul Aziz Ibn Saud and was officially proclaimed fully sovereign on September 22, 1932.

Ibn Saud, the founder of Saudi Arabia, was the "Imam" of his people, as well as the King. This meant that he lead them as an example of religious devotion. His private life was strictly disciplined according to Muslim code. King Abdul Aziz did not like to be addressed as "King" or "Your Majesty." He constantly reminded Saudis that the Kingdom belongs to God, and that Majesty is an attribute of Allah. He loved hunting, either with hawks or, as later became the fashion, shooting from open cars careening across the desert.[6] Abdul Aziz (Ibn Saud) was a unique and extraordinary mixture. He was blessed with charm and sensitivity to which a Westerner found it easy to respond. Animated by deep Islamic conviction and believing in his mission to lead the Wahhabi guidance in the twentieth century, he was a consummate politician. He died on November 9, 1953, in Taif.[7]

Saudi Arabia is the only country in the world named after its founder and ruler. The name in Arabic is "Almamlakah Alarabia Al-Saudia," which literally means the Arabian Kingdom of the House of Saud.

There are many sons of Ibn Saud. Currently, members of the Royal Family hold positions in the government at all

[5]The U.S. did not formally recognize the existence of the Saudi state until May, 1931, five years after Britain and the U.S.S.R.

[6]Peter Mansfield, *The New Arabians* (Chicago: J.C. Fergusons Publishing Co., 1981), p. 17

[7]The history of modern Saudi Arabia begins with Abdul Aziz Al-Saud, known to the West as Ibn Saud.

levels. For completeness we include Table 1 (see page 23), which shows the key members of the Royal Family of King Abdul Aziz Ibn Saud.

2. Geographical Location

The Kingdom is bounded on the north by Jordan, Iraq, and Kuwait, on the east by the Arabian Gulf, Qatar, United Arab Emirates, and the Sultanate of Oman. To the west, it is bounded by the Red Sea, and to the south by Yemen and South Yemen. It is separated from Africa by the Red Sea and from Asia by the Arabian Gulf. In the southeast is the Empty Quarter or the "Rub'al-Khali," which is the largest continuous body of sand in the world, with dunes rising to a height of 500 feet or more, occupying an area of about 250,000 square miles. A tract of deep, shifting sand the size of Texas, the Empty Quarter stretches from the inner margins of the Yemen highlands to the mountain chains of Oman and to a huge salt quicksand called "Um-as-Summ" or "Mother of Poison." In addition, there is no vegetation, nor any permanent inhabitants in "Rub'al-Khali." Even the nomads and their camels have a hard time surviving. It is now known that "Rub'al-Khali" went through a less arid phase some 3,000 years ago, and that it is the largest desert in the world.

The total area of the Kingdom is 900,000 square miles, which is slightly less than one-third the size of the United States. It occupies four-fifths of the Arabian Peninsula.

The Kingdom of Saudi Arabia is the largest country in the world with no major rivers and few streams.

3. Government

Arabic is the official language in the Kingdom,[8] although English is frequently spoken in the business communities of Dhahran, Alkhobar, Dammam, Jubail, Jeddah, Yanbu, Riyadh, Abha, Taif and Khamis Mushayat.

The government is a monarchy.[9] Executive and legislative authority is exercised by the King and Council of Ministers within the framework of Islamic law. Saudi Arabia is one of the few states to use the Qur'an as its constitution.

King Fahd Ibn Abdul Aziz Al-Saud, assisted by the Royal Cabinet, is the center of all the political activity. He is the Head of Government and Chief of State.[10] The Cabinet is stable, and most of the Ministers are young and highly educated.

Political parties, trade unions, demonstrations, and various interest groups are not permitted in Saudi Arabia. Saudis believe unions are unnecessary, since the law is fully protective of the workers.

The Saudi leadership insists that the very essence of the

[8]Interestingly, Arabic is written from right to left, except the numbers. The numbers used in the Western world are of Arabic origin, whereas the numbers used in Arabic countries originated in India. Arabic is a language that lends itself to poetic expression. It contains a vast store of vocabulary that is unique in its capacity to express both a grandiose idea, and at the same time, the subtlest nuance.

[9]The principle of succession by age among the Royal Family is practiced in Saudi Arabia.

[10]Table 2 shows the Royal Cabinet of Saudi Arabia as of November, 1984. The Cabinet has doubled in size since 1975, in order to better deal with the Kingdom's development plans.

Kingdom's political system is Islam.[11] This is especially true since Islam has given life to the State from the mid-eighteenth century to the present. This has meant that the religious leaders (Ulama) have played an influential role in the government of Saudi Arabia. Their influence is manifested through the implementation of the rules of Islam, the judicial system of the country, and religious jurisprudence. These religious leaders are also active in preaching and in religious guidance groups, with affiliated offices all over the Kingdom. They are responsible for the supervision of all mosques and of religious and Islamic legal education at all levels, including the education of girls in the Kingdom.[12]

The "Shari'ah," the Islamic Code of Justice based on the Qur'an, is the basis of the legal system of the Kingdom. Islam makes no distinction between religious and civil law. The Qur'an, however, does not contain all the rules which are necessary in all circumstances. The Muslims therefore look beyond it to the sayings of the Prophet, called the "Hadith,[13]" and the "Sunnah" (the example of Prophet Mohammed; i.e., his personal acts or sayings).

The Saudi Royal Family, Al-Saud, has continued to play an historic role in the life of the Arab Peninsula and the

---

[11]The Islamic political system is egalitarian and based on social justice and service to people.

[12]*Ibid*, p. 67.

[13]"Hadith": The first generation of Muslims committed the Hadith to memory and, over the years, the sayings were tested for provenance, classified, and published. The Hadith range from religious instruction, speech, the law, social and moral teaching, encompassing every facet of human experience. An example of the Hadith is "Pay the worker before his sweat dries."

neighboring regions as well.[14] In addition, the descendants of Mohammad Ibn Abdul Wahab became known after his death as "Al-Sheikh," and they preserve their separate identity in the Kingdom to this day.

Saudi leadership has the special status in the Muslim world as the guardian of the two holy cities of Makkah and Medina.

The Kingdom follows an independent foreign policy and plays a leading role in the Arab and Muslim world because of its unique religious and financial position.

The Saudi policy, from King Abdul Aziz to King Fahd, has been characterized by shrewdness and intelligence of thought, and has permanently adhered to the following obligations and moral necessities:[15]

— Ceaseless efforts for the country's internal construction.
— Striving for Islamic solidarity.
— Struggle for the consolidation of Arab fraternal relations.
— Positive contribution to world peace and international understanding.

In the arena of international politics, Saudi Arabia, as a founding member of the United Nations, has played an important part in the activities of the related international bodies and special agencies. Saudi embassies, consulates,

[14]Saudi Arabia has been blessed with two very strong kings in Abdul Aziz and Faisal. See Appendix 6. The House of Saud enjoys considerable popularity at this stratum of Saudi society. The political strength of the House of Saud is ultimately derived from the fact that it has been woven into the religious and social fabric of the Kingdom.

[15]Ministry of Information, Riyadh, Saudi Arabia, 1983.

and representatives all over the world have had a significant role in strengthening the ties of friendship and cooperation between the Kingdom and friendly nations.

Saudi Arabia has never been colonized by another country. It maintains political ties with the United States, and of course, the Kingdom's oil serves the vital national interest of the U.S.[16]

More importantly, the Saudi government is reluctant to establish diplomatic ties with the Soviet Union, unless actual benefits of such relations can be agreed upon, because Saudis possess a basic fear and mistrust of Communism.

In fact, before Saudi Arabia will improve relations with the Soviets, the following conditions must be met.

— Withdrawal of all Soviet forces from Afghanistan.
— An end to all hostile Soviet propaganda against the Kingdom.
— A reduction of Soviet military presence in the region, particularly in South Yemen.
— Greater freedom for Soviet Muslims to practice their religion.

If the Soviets meet the above conditions, the Saudi policy-makers will not necessarily exchange ambassadors, because the proper "psychological climate" must also exist.[17]

The principle Saudi foreign policy goal is to preserve

[16]The concept of national interest as used here refers to the articulation of national policies which insure the protection of national security and the promotion of the economic and social well-being of all Americans. Significantly, Saudi purchases of U.S. goods and services, for example, have climbed from well under a billion dollars per year as recently as ten years ago to between eight and nine billion dollars annually in each of the last several years.

[17]*Christian Science Monitor*, May 9, 1984, p. 14.

Islamic values in Saudi Arabia and the Muslim world in general. Saudi leadership seeks to accomplish this with the cooperation of the Western powers against Communism and radicalism.

4. Population

The majority of Saudi Arabians are descended from Arab tribes indigenous to the Peninsula. Other ethnic populations have originated from Muslims of other countries and regions who, after making their pilgrimage to Saudi Arabia, decided to settle there.

Saudi Arabia today is underpopulated. Its population is estimated at nearly seven million people; most of them are farmers or townspeople, and only 12 percent are nomads (Bedouins). Physically, the majority of the people are slender, dark-eyed, and olive-skinned, with wavy black hair.[18] See Table 3 (page 28) for distribution of total population in Saudi Arabia.

The Bedouins are nomadic tribes, their mode of living depending upon flocks of sheep, goats, or camel herds. Each Bedouin tribe is governed by a chief, or elder, selected by the male members of the tribe. There are 85 major tribes in Saudi Arabia, as shown in Table 4 (see page 29). The term "Bedouin," or "Badawi," in Arabic, is used mainly by townsfolk to refer to the "tent-dweller."

The tribal chief, or the elder, "speaks for" the tribe. He is also responsible for the tribe's external relations.

The Southern and Northern Bedouins have always had different customs. Those of the south dress differently, and

[18]The large influx of Africans in past through the trade and pilgrimages has resulted in a certain portion of Negroes in the population.

in their migrations do not live in tents, but merely hang a sunshade from a tree, or go between mountain caves and camps. The Bedouins of the north ride their camels on saddles, while the southern Bedouins ride without saddles.

The tribes of the northern part of Saudi Arabia believe that Bedouin ways are best, and that the desert made the Bedouins what they are. Allah sends the rain so that the herds will have pasture; from the herds the Bedouins have milk to drink, skins to build their tents, and young animals to sell in exchange for grain and coffee. Furthermore, in the Arab Peninsula, wars between Bedouin tribes and raids on settled communities were common and were celebrated in a poetic tradition, so that by the sixth century they had helped establish a classic literary Arabic language.

However, Bedouins are becoming fewer in number in the Saudi society; government subsidies and Toyota pickups are now the dominant elements of the modern Saudi nomads.

Menfolk in modern-day Bedouin tribes are herders or hunters who continue to engage in falconry, the training of "saluki" hunting dogs, and the breeding of the world-famous Arabian stallions.

The settled and nomadic sectors of Saudi society obviously differ greatly in their economic pursuits and in the social patterns of daily life. They share to a remarkable degree, however, a common body of social values. For example, some differences in the dress of Bedouin women and town women exist, but the major factor which determines the type of dress and social customs followed by Saudi women seems to be the socio-economic standing of their families.

The people of Saudi Arabia have a great love for their language. Arabic is the official language of the Kingdom, and the major dialects are described below:

Hejazi—This dialect is spoken in the Western Province of the Kingdom (Jeddah, Taif and the Holy Cities of Makkah and Medina). The Hejazi dialect is used for governmental and commercial purposes; it has become the most widely used dialect in the Arabian Peninsula. In this dialect, one finds words that have been borrowed from other dialects, such as Egyptian, Palestinian, and Jordanian.

Najdi—The Najdi dialect is spoken in and around Riyadh, in the north central part of the country. The Najdi dialect enjoys prestige by virtue of its conservatism and relative closeness to classical Arabic, and because it is the dialect of the Royal Family.

Sharqi—This dialect is spoken in the oil-rich eastern region.

These dialects are not radically different from each other. People speaking these various dialects have no problem in understanding or communicating with each other, just as people in the northern U.S. have no difficulty communicating with people of the southern regions.

5. Currency

Saudi Arabia established its independent monetary system in 1928; the unit of currency is the *riyal*, which is subdivided into 100 *halalahs*.[19] The first official paper currency did not appear until 1961, when the government

---

[19]$1.00 U.S. was equal to 3.50 Saudi Riyals in May, 1984.

issued notes in denominations of one, two, five, ten, fifty
and one-hundred *riyals*. Coins are in 5, 10, 25, 50 and 100
denominations. The *riyals* are quoted in dollars, but based on
Special Drawing Rights (SDR). As the SDR/dollar rate
varies, so the official *riyal*/dollar rate is revalued at intervals
to keep within a narrow band around SDR 1 = SR 4.28.

6. *Provinces of the Kingdom of Saudi Arabia*

The administration of Saudi provinces is in the hands of
fourteen governors. These men are the direct representatives of the King. They are part of the Ministry of the
Interior and are quite powerful.

Geographically, the country is divided into Administrative District/Provinces or major regions.[20]

Asir is the Kingdom's summer resort area, which
includes the major cities of Abha, Khamis Mushate, Najran
and Jizan. Asir is the relatively fertile strip of coastal moun-
tains in the extreme southwest, with peaks up to 10,000 feet
high. In the region, fruit, vegetables and other crops can be
grown on a large scale. Asir means "the difficult region,"
but it is the one well-watered region of Saudi Arabia. The
rainfall has allowed southwesterners to live a settled life as
cultivators of the soil and as herdsmen.

Al-Hejaz is an area of about 80,000 square miles. The
origins and distribution of the Hejazi people have been
strongly influenced by geography. As an area well-suited
for commerce, it has experienced the effects of trade and
conquest through the centuries. The region encompasses
the balance of the west coast, with the mountain chain

---

[20]Empty Quarter is not included herein.

decreasing somewhat in height toward the north, and the coastal plain bordering the Red Sea widening slightly. Located here is the busy port of Jeddah, the country's major business center. Jeddah, one of the world's oldest cities, has a population of 1.5 million. Jeddah means "grandmother" in Arabic. The city is also the most cosmopolitan, for it is the point of entry for pilgrims on their way to the holy shrines of Mecca and Medina, visited by over a million pilgrims each year. Although the word *hejaz* means "barrier," the history of the area and its people belies the term. The barrier referred to is the Great Escarpment which runs along, rather than across, the country.

The province of Najd is the heart and cradle of the country. At its center is Riyadh, the rapidly-growing industrial capital of the Kingdom. *Al-riyadh* means "the garden' in Arabic. Its inhabitants (Najdis) are a gifted and remarkable people. From their nomadic past they have inherited an innate inner compass, as well as deep pride and self-respect. Their basic conservatism and their attachment to traditional ways and ideals remain strong.

Al-Hasa, or the Eastern Province as it is commonly known, is the area which produces crude oil and natural gas for export. Aramco headquarters are in this region, in Dhahran; Ras Tanuma is the world's largest petroleum port. Dammam, Dhahran and Al-Khobar are fast growing into consolidated metropolitan areas. Al-Hasa also has a number of oases including Hardah, Hofuf and Qatif. Date palms and other crops are grown at these locations.

The climate is one of the major influences of life in the eastern provinces. The year can be divided into three seasons; the cool season, during the months of December through March, the hot season, when daytime temperatures can reach 110° Fahrenheit, and the transitional months of April, May, October, and November which are still relatively hot, but less humid. The humidity, especially in the coastal areas, causes the temperature to feel cooler in the winter and hotter in the summer.

Rainfall is minimal, but occasional heavy rainstorms may occur between November and March. Temperatures in the northern region of the Kingdom range from very hot in the summer to chilly days during winter months. A typical summer daytime temperature can reach 125° Fahrenheit. Humidity is low all year. The wind blows constantly, occasionally developing into sandstorms called "Shamal."[21]

Weather on the west coast is similar to that of Jeddah; humidity is high during the hot months (April-September), with some rainfull during the winter months.

7. The Five Pillars of Islam

Saudi Arabia is the country where Islam originated, and all Saudi citizens are Muslims. Islam means submission to the will of God. The language of the Qur'an is Arabic. The Qur'an is the Muslim Holy Book and is considered to be Allah's revelation to the prophet Muhammad; it contains 114 chapters.

Muslims honor Christianity and Judaism as divinely-inspired faiths; they also believe that these religions have been superceded as well as succeeded by Islam.[22]

---

[21]"Shamal" is a common occurrence. Usually, these sandstorms are of short duration. However, at other times these storms may last for days.

[22]Judaism was the first monotheistic religion in the Middle East. Muslims believe that Jesus was sent to further people's belief in God rather than idols. When not everyone converted to these beliefs, God sent the Prophet Muhammad.

Although Islam has become better known in the West, it is still misunderstood by many Westerners. How many Westerners realize that Muslims revere Jesus as a prophet? (The name for Jesus in Arabic is "'Issa.") In the Muslim view, Jesus was, like all prophets, a human being. Abraham, Moses, Jesus, Muhammad, and all other prophets are equal in Muslim faith and consideration. It is written in the Qur'an that a Muslim shall not discriminate between any of the Prophets of Allah.[23]

Muslims believe prophets were sent by God (Allah) to the people prior to Muhammad, and that the Prophet is the "last and greatest Prophet." Muhammad, the last Messenger of Allah to mankind, defined Islam as follows:

> "Islam is to acknowledge that there is no god but Allah and that Muhammad is His messenger, to perform prayers, pay the poor tax (Zakat), fast the month of Ramadan and to do pilgrimage to the Holy House of Makkah if you have the means for it."[24]

Therefore, every Muslim is expected to observe a set of religious duties known collectively as the Five Pillars of Islam (Ibadat).[25]

The Five Pillars of Islam are summarized below:

(1) The Profession of Faith (Shahadah), by which a person becomes a Muslim. This individual simply repeats an Arabic phrase which means, "There is no god but Allah and Muhammad is his messenger." Significantly, no other words are heard or repeated more frequently throughout the life of devoted Muslims than these. They occur in the

[23]This is stated at the end of the first Sura of Baqarah. Author's translation.
[24]Abdul Rahman Bin Hamad Al-Omar, *Islam: The Religion of Truth* (Riyadh: Alfarazdak Press, Riydah, 1395 H), p. 17.
[25]It is perhaps necessary to indicate that the sects of Islam have differed amongst themselves not on matters of theology so much as on questions of practice.

summons of the Muezzin (Mu'adhin) to prayer, chanting several times a day from the minaret of the mosque. Therefore, a Shahadah constitutes the first major requirement for becoming a Muslim.

(2) Prayer (Salat) which must be performed five times a day as follows:[26] dawn (*fajr*), noon (*duhr*), afternoon (*assr*), sunset (*maghreb*), and night (*i'sha*).

The worshipper must face the holy city of Makkah and repeat prayers in Arabic, regardless of the native language. Praying five times a day is considered the backbone of Islamic religion.

Muslim men are required to participate in public prayer at noon on Fridays (the Muslim holy day), when the congregation of worshippers may be addressed by an "Imam" or religious leader. Women used to attend public prayer at the time of the Prophet, but it later became a tradition for them to pray at home. However, in the modern era, many mosques reserve places for women.

(3) Payment of a charitable tax (*zakat*). Traditionally, the amount to be paid averages two-and-a-half percent of one's income. *Zakat* is very much a personal obligation, and it is thus very difficult for the state to monitor its collection effectively.

Allah enjoined Muslims to cooperate with one another in material and moral fields. *Zakat* is a form of this cooperation. It is the duty of Muslims to wish for their fellow-brothers what they wish for themselves, and to dislike for them what they dislike for themselves.

There are major situations where *zakat* is applicable

[26] A Muslim may pray at home, in any mosque or in the open air of the desert. Before prayer, however, the Muslim should cleanse himself with pure water, removing all traces of stool, urine, or any other dirt. In this way, he purifies himself physically and morally.

relative to the ownership of animals, gold, silver, articles of trade, and of the produce of the land. The revenue thus collected is used to help the poor of the Islamic community. The Qur'an is specific as to those who are eligible to receive the alms distributed under *zakat* provisions. "The free will offerings are for the poor and needy, those who work to collect them, the travelers; so God ordains."[27]

(4) Fast (The Sawm). It takes place during the ninth month of Islam's calendar (Ramadan).[28] The Qur'an prescribes fasting, "as it was prescribed for those who were before you." During the month of Ramadan, a Muslim is not permitted to partake of food and drink, or to engage in sexual relations, during the day.

Exceptions to required fasting are the sick, feeble, those traveling on caravans, and soldiers fighting in war. Fasting is a time for consideration of those less fortunate, for reading the Qur'an, and for prayer. When the sun sets on the last evening of Ramadan, the Islamic world joins in the feast of "Eid Alfiter," in glorious celebration of the end of the fast. Streets in Muslim countries take on a festive look, with throngs of people moving from one house to another. Muslims "congratulate" one another on this festival day with "Eid Mubarak."

(5) The Pilgrimage (Hajj). Every male Muslim who can afford it and who is physically capable is expected to undertake a visit to the Holy City of Makkah, Prophet Muhammad's birthplace, and to Medina, the Prophet's burial place. Pilgrimage is normally performed during the twelfth

[27]John L. Esposito, *Islam and Development: Religion and Socio-Political Change* (Syracuse, N.Y.: Syracuse University Press, 1980), p. 28.

[28]The date on which Ramadan begins may vary from the calendar date. It actually starts only after the new moon is sighted.

month of the year (Dhul-Hijjah). Women may also undertake a pilgrimage, but women must be accompanied by a
proper male escort.

The "Eid Al-Adha," the greater of the two major Islamic
festivals, occurs during Dhul-Hijjah; the other major festival is "Eid Alfter." Eid Al-Adha marks the completion of
"Hajj" and is observed with the sacrifice of an animal
(usually a lamb) to commemorate Abraham's sacrifice. The
animal is then divided into three equal portions; one for the
use of the family, one for the neighbors, and one for the
poor.

Significantly, the Hajj places a special burden on the
government to insure that the millions of pilgrims can be
accommodated and worship. Pilgrims from every corner of
the globe assemble at the same place and perform the same
ritual, while wearing identical garments.

More than three million people made the Hajj in 1983.
This figure represents the intensity with which Muslims
regard the holy shrines. Historically, the first pilgrimage
was made by the prophet Abraham, his wife Hagar, and son
Ishmael. Once at Mecca, Abraham and Ishmael built the
Ka'aba, a stone cube toward which Muslims face while
praying. (See Appendix 5).

From a religious perspective, the main differences
between Islam and Christianity are their views of the super-
natural, their exclusiveness, and their theological orientation. The two are more similar than different, and the
differences are not doctrinal but functional.[29]

Prophet Muhammad was born in 571 AD into the
House of Hashim of the Quaraish tribe. He was raised by

[29]Edward Said and Faud Sulieman, *The Arab Today: Alternative for Tomorrow*
(Columbus, Ohio: Forum Associate, Inc., 1973), p. 29.

an uncle, Abu-Talib. When he was twenty-six years old, he married the wealthy widow Khadija, who was several years his senior. Khadija was an astute businesswoman who engaged in the conduct of her late husband's caravan commerce. They had four daughters who survived to maturity, and several sons, none of whom lived to adulthood.[30]

Muhammad's message began at age forty, when the Angel Gabriel revealed the Qur'an to him.[31] The leaders of Makkah opposed Islam, but when the Prophet died in 632 AD, nearly all the Arabian peninsula accepted Islam.

To a Muslim, Islam is an integral part of daily life, helping to make an ordered society in which man's spiritual, political, and economic status is clearly set out. Islam is not only a set of spiritual beliefs and rituals; it is also a social order, a philosophy of life, and a system of economic rules and government. Muslim groups do differ, however, on the degree of interplay between Islam and nationalism.

The two major sects of Islam are the Sunni and the Shi'ah; the mystic tradition in Islam is Sufism. A Sufi adept believes he has acquired a special inner knowledge direct from Allah. Muslims believe God is the creator of the universe. Allah created man and woman to worship him and to act toward other people in certain ways.

The Qur'an places great emphasis upon the Almighty power of Allah and man's obligation to recognize his utter dependence upon the Creator Allah as the "Compassionate and Merciful One." Man is seen as God's highest creation,

[30]See Alfred Guillaume, *The Life of Mohammad* (Oxford: Oxford University Press, 1955).

[31]It became Muhammad's custom to retreat for mediation at a hillside cave on the outskirts of Makkah. In the year 610 AD, he received his call (Alwahi) to preach the truth concerning God (Allah) to his fellow Meccans.

but limited and sinful. God gave the Qur'an to Muhammad to guide men to the truth; those who repent and sincerely submit to God return to a state of sinlessness. In the end, the sinless go to paradise, a place of physical and spiritual pleasure, and the wicked burn in Hell.[32]

Belief in the hereafter and the Day of Judgment is among the doctrines of Islam. The world is seen as a place of trial and each man is to be judged on the basis of the life he lives in it. According to the Qur'an, each man shall be his own judge:

> And every man's deed have we
> fastened about his neck; and on the day
> of Resurrection will we bring
> forthwith to him a book which
> shall be proffered to him wide
> open: Read your book: there
> need be none but your self
> to make out an account against
> you this day (Chapter 17:14-15)[33]

According to the Qur'an, human beings are God's representatives on earth, and as such have the right to acquire property and wealth to fulfill personal needs and social responsibilities. However, not all methods of gaining wealth are acceptable.

The concepts of private property and individual responsibility are basic to Islamic thought on human dignity. They

[32]The Qur'an challenges believers to follow the example of the Prophet Muhammad, who is described as the noble paradigm. Since one of Muhammad's achievements was to lay the foundations of a state based on Islamic teachings, Muslims have a duty to follow his example in this respect as well.
[33]Author's translation.

are also viewed as key to the production of economic wealth, which in turn is a key to implementing the highly sophisticated and ambitious Saudi plans for social justice.

8. Islamic Calendar

The Islamic calendar, often referred to as Muhammadan, is a lunar reckoning from the year of Muhammad's flight (Hijra). The first day of the month of "Muharram" marks the beginning of the Islamic calendar. This is New Year's Day. It commemorates the day the Prophet Muhammad emigrated from Makkah to Medina (Hijra) and established the first mosque and the Islamic community. This trip took place in 622 AD.[34]

The Muslim calendar is calculated according to the orbiting of the moon around the earth. A month is counted from the new moon to the next new moon. Since the average interval between the consecutive similar phases of the moon is 29 days, 12 hours, and 44 minutes, with a variation of half a day, a lunar month consists of either 29 or 30 days. Taking this into account, there are an extra 44 minutes each month which add up to 11 days every 30 years. Therefore, it was agreed to have eleven leap years within each thirty-year period. This is not noticeable, as the months are either twenty-nine or thirty days.

---

[34]This is considered the most important date for Muslims because it signifies the birth of the Islamic faith.

The twelve Islamic months that constitute the lunar year are listed below:

1. Maharram[35]
2. Safar
3. Rabi' Awal
4. Rabi 'Thani
5. Jamad Awal
6. Jamad Thani

7. Rajab
8. Sha'aban
9. Ramadan
10. Shawal
11. Dhul Qu'dah
12. Dhul-Hijjah

Muslims believe that Allah created the night before the day. Thus, the night of the 27th of the month refers to the night preceding the 27th day of the month, and the night of Friday is the night preceding Friday, i.e., Thursday after sunset.

The beginning of the new month depends on the sighting of the new noon by the naked eye a few minutes after sunset on the evening of the 29th day of the month. If the new moon is sighted on that evening, the next day will be the first of the new month. If the new moon is not sighted that evening, the next day will be the 30th of the month and the day after that will be the first day of the new month. The person who has sighted the moon must be a Muslim and must have two adult witnesses to go with him before the town's religious leader.

This results in many difficulties for determining the exact dates of Muslim festivals in advance.

[35] "Ashura" (the first ten days of Muharram), is observed by Shiite Muslims, a small minority group living mostly in the Eastern Province of the Kingdom. It marks the climax of ten days' lamentation for the murder of Hussain, a grandson of Prophet Muhammad and a great leader of his day. These ten days are of mourning, penance, and self-flagellation.

TABLE 1
KEY MEMBERS OF THE FAMILY OF
KING ABDUL AZIZ IBN SAUD

Abdul Aziz Ibn Saud	born 1876; ruled 1902-53; died 1953
Saud	born 1902; ruled 1953-1964; died 1975
Faisal	born 1906; ruled 1964-1975; died 1975
The Sons of King Faisal	
-Abdallah	born 1921; former Minister of Interior
-Khalid	born 1941; Governor of Asir
-Mohammad	born 1937; President, Islamic Bank
-Saud	born 1941; Foreign Minister since 1975
-Abd-al-Rahman	born 1942; Armed Forces
-Turki	born 1945; Intelligence
Mohammad	born 1910
Khalid	born 1912; ruled 1975; died June June 12, 1982
Nasir	born 1920; former Governor of Riyadh until 1974; died September, 1984.
Sa'ad	born 1920

Musa'id	born 1923
Abd al-Muhsin	born 1925; Governor of Medina
Fahad	born 1921; ruled June 1982 to present
Sultan	born 1924; Minister of Defense and Aviation and Inspectate General; Second Deputy Premier
Abd al-Rahman	born 1926; Vice Minister of Defense
Nayif	born 1933; Minister of Interior since 1975
Turki	born 1934; Vice Minister of Defense until 1978
Salman	born 1936; Governor of Riyadh
Ahmad	born 1940; Deputy Minister of Interior
Abdullah	born 1923; National Guard and Crown Prince; First Deputy Premier
Fawwaz	born 1934; former Governor of Makkah
Bandar	born 1923; Noted for strict religious observance
Mish'al	born 1926; former Governor of Makkah and Minister of Defense from 1951-1956

Mit'ab	born 1928; Minister of Public Works and Housing
Talal	born 1931; The United Nations
Nawwaf	born 1934; head of Royal palace under Saud
Badr	born 1933; Deputy Commander of the National Guard
Abdelillah	born 1935; Governor of Qassim
Abd al-Majid	born 1940; Governor of Tabuk
Majid	born 1934; Governor of Mecca; former Minister of Municipal Affairs
Sattam	born 1943; Deputy Governor of Riyadh
Muqrin	burn 1943; Governor of Hail since 1980
Mumduh	born 1941
Hidhlul	born 1941
Mashhur	born 1942
Hamoud	born 1947

Source: Alvin J. Cottrell, *The Persian Gulf States* (Baltimore: The John Hopkins University Press, 1980), pp. 172-183; and various Saudi Arabian newspapers translated by the author (1984).

TABLE 2

THE ROYAL CABINET OF THE KINGDOM (1984)

Prince Abdullah Ibn Abdul Aziz*	First Deputy Premier, Crown Prince, and Commander of the National Guard
Prince Sultan Ibn Abdul Aziz*	Second Deputy Premier and Minister of Defense and Aviation and General Inspectorate
Prince Saud Al Faisal*	Foreign Affairs
Mohammad Ali Abalkhail	Finance and National Economy
Ahmed Zaki Yamani	Petroleum and Minerals
Prince Nayif Ibn Abdul Aziz*	Interior
Sheikh Ali Al-Shaer	Information
Abdul Aziz Al-Zamil	Industry and Electricity
Solaiman Al Solaim	Commerce
Prince Moti'b Ibn Abdul Aziz*	Public Works and Housing
Hassan Ibn Abdullah Al-Sheikh*	Higher Education
Ibrahim Ibn Mohammad Al-Sheikh**	Justice
Hussein Ibrahim Al-Mansouri	Communication

Abdelaziz Abdullah Al-Khuwaiter	Education
Hisham Muhaildin Nazir	Planning
Abdulwahab Ahmed Abdelwasi	Pilgrimage Affairs and Awqaf
Abdul-rahman Ibn Abdulaziz Al-Sheikh**	Agriculture and Water
Alawi Darwish Kayyal	Post, Telegraph and Telecommunications
Mohammad Ibrahim Masoud	Minister of State
Mohammad Abdullatif Al-Mihim	Minister of State
Prince Faisal Ibn Fahd*	President of Youth Welfare
Fayez Badr	Minister without portfolio
Abdulahdi Hassan Tahr	Governor of PETROMIN
Faisal A. Al-Hejalan	Minister of Health
Ibrahim Al-Angari	Municipalities and Rural Affairs
Mohammad Ali Fayez	Labor and Social Affairs

*Member of the Royal Family.
**Al-Sheikh: They remain one of the four families with whom the Al-Saud intermarry; they are second only to the Royal Family in the Council of Ministers; and they also hold important positions in the police and Armed Forces.

Source: This information was obtained by the author from various Saudi Arabian newspapers. The spelling of the names may vary.

TABLE 3

DISTRIBUTION OF TOTAL POPULATION IN SAUDI ARABIA
(7 million)

Category	Percentage
Living in Metropolitan Centers (population more than 100,000)	42
Living in Small Towns	12
Living in Rural Areas	46

Source: Ministry of Planning Estimates, 1984.

TABLE 4
NAMES OF MAJOR TRIBES IN THE KINGDOM

Belahmer

Belasmer

Ahle Bareg[q]

Bahr bin Sukayna

Baqum

Bili

Bano Tamim

Bano Thawa'h

Thamalah

Thaqif

Al Gadadlah

Go'dah

Gohaynah

Belhareth

Kabilat al Howaytat

Asir

Al Kam al Howle

Al Ashraf

Quaraysh

Bano Malek

Al Masarehah

Kabilat al Morrah

Al Mongehah

Al Nogo'a

Amre

Kabilat Bani Hager

Hothayl

Kath'am

Kotha'ah

Kamiseen

Bano Kidayr

Al-Aldorayeb

D'akyah

Sawasir

Rabiy'ah

Rigal al Ma'a

Al Rashaydah

Al Raysh

Zahran

Bano Zeid

Saby'a

Bano Sa'ad

Sufyan

Al Sahol

Al Shararat

Kabilat Fahme

Belgarn

Bano Malek Asir

Bano Muhammad

Me'gyed

Al Mosa

Bano Nashar

Bal'eyre

Kabilat Bani Hager

Helal

Bano Ya'ly

Kabilat al Ogman

Kabilat Harb

Kailat al Howaytat

Ahle Hala

Thoo Hasan

Khaled

Shamran

Bano Shehre

Shahran

Al Sah'lawah

Shammar

Kabilat Twoowayreg[q]

Al Zufayer

Kabilat Anzah

Kabilat Utaybah

Kabilat Bani Atayah

Al Awazim

Bano Abse

Bano Shobayl

Qahtan*

Al Mahdy

Bano Marwan

Kabilat Motayer

Al Manasir

Nagran

Al Nomoor

Gamid

Hotaym

Yam

Source: Fouad Al-Farsy, *Saudi Arabia: A Case Study in Development,* (London: Stacey International, 1980), p. 78.
*Qahtan is the largest single tribe in the Kingdom.

PART TWO

CULTURAL AND RELIGIOUS PERSPECTIVE

1. Traditions and Values of the Saudis

Following my arrival in the Kingdom of Saudi Arabia in 1979, I worked with people of several nationalities as a training director. It was in this position that I realized there was a great need for a book in the English language about the values, traditions, and Islamic laws in the Kingdom. I had the opportunity to attend various lectures and cultural presentations in the United States, and the information presented was outdated and inaccurate, mainly relating to the pre-oil discovery period. In light of this lack of information, I felt that such a book would be of great value, and that it should be written in such a way that non-Arabic speaking people would be able to enjoy and appreciate the insights of a scholar who is familiar with Saudi society and Islam.

Culture is a unique aspect of mankind. It reflects how we differ from other people as well as from the animal world. Human behavior is a product of very complex learning processes that take place within a cultural context.[1]

Culture is not merely the reflection of our individual personalities or our particular sets of eccentricities. It may

---

[1]James F. Downs, *Cultures in Crisis,* (Beverly Hills, California: Glencoe Press, 1971) p. 29.

be defined as the shared explanations for events and actions and the prescribed responses to specific situations which we hold in common with others who are part of our group, tribe, nation, social class, or other collectivity. A person's culture will greatly influence his experiences and perceptions of life overseas.

Motivations for moving overseas are varied. An overseas assignment is a normal part of a career in international business, the foreign service, or the military; people who pursue such careers may not even question the need for such travel. For others, moving overseas contains a large measure of uncertainty and a search for meaning and significance in life. However, some element of dissatisfaction with one's own culture probably plays a part in one's decision to choose the complicated, demanding and itinerant existence of living overseas.[2]

In the West, the Arab is frequently presented as a menace or terrorist, a shadowy figure who operates outside an acceptable value system and is therefore to be feared and mistrusted. It is also felt, by Western standards, that the Arabs are weak and have low self-esteem. Arabs are viewed as schizophrenic, confused, and heartless.

The West, which exerts a tremendous influence in Arab life, continues to belittle, intimidate, and denigrate the Arab people. In the words of William Hazlitt, "Prejudice is the child of ignorance; not all images are true."[3]

---

[2]George V. Coelho and Pual I. Ahmed, *Uprooting and Development: Dilemmas Coping With Modernization* (New York: Plenum Press, 1980), p. 23.

[3]George M. Atiyeh, *Arab and American Cultures* (Washington, D.C.: American Enterprise Institute for Public Policy Research, 1979), p. 142.

Consequently, the Arab sense of humor and charm, the artfulness of the Arab mind, the sensitivity and cordiality of the Arab nature, as well as the creative imagination of the Arab soul, are not perceived by the Westerner due to this heavy veil of misinterpretation.

This chapter takes the reader on a journey into daily Saudi life, revealing how the Islamic religion plays a vital role in the nation's entire government, as well as in everyday social customs, such as the almost complete segregation of the sexes and the prescription of what one is allowed or forbidden to do in society.

"My people and my land are yours." Today, centuries later, this traditional Saudi Arabian greeting has been shortened to "people and land" (*Ahlan Wa Sahlan*). But this welcome evokes wonder. What kind of gesture or expression is it that comes from a host in whose country a man's word is a solemn vow? Such a society started early in man's memory and today consists of thought patterns and behavior which can only evolve from the total experience shared by a unique group of people over time.[4] So it is in the Kingdom of Saudi Arabia.

Traditional rules still exist which include how a man is to become successful in life, the importance of plural marriage (an institution that still thrives), and the importance of having many children. All of these rules are in turn related to the rules of treating elders with proper respect and attention.[5]

Social customs are not changed automatically by factors

[4]Man is viewed as the controlled product of society and culture, and yet also as the maker of society and culture.
[5]Marvin Harris, *The Rise of Anthropological Theory*. (New York: Harper and Row, 1968), p. 601.

of urban living and industrial employment. Urban living is one of the traditional life styles of Saudi Arabia. It is nothing new, although now it is much more common for a villager or nomad to move to the city.

Traditionally, the Saudi Arabian family was a miniature society in itself. It was the financial security system, the insurance program, the unemployment and disaster relief organization, the major entertainment network and the source of love, honor and joy. A large family worked closely together to help and support each member. While this is still true today, the system has been greatly modified as the Saudis have become more mobile and as housing for individual families has become more available.

A Saudi derives his identity and status from the family to which he or she belongs. Several thousand Saudis may take pride in belonging to the Royal Family, but the other seven million citizens of the Kingdom also identify themselves by family, tribe and region.

The family has a prominent role in socialization and the development of basic personality traits and values.[6] Loyalty and duty to the family are greater than any other obligation of society or business. In more general terms, the extended family is not only the primary unit in which Saudis live or maintain a home, it is also the pillar of society. Communal cohesion is undoubtedly the most desired value within the Saudi value system.

Significantly, the essence of family unity extends to grandparents, aunts, uncles, and cousins. Many houses

---

[6]In socialization among Arabs, sexual differences between boys and girls are stressed. The attitude toward sex is generally repressive, and the children do not receive sex education or instructions about sexual matters, because it is forbidden.

include relatives from outside the immediate family who do not have their own home.

The status of the individual in Saudi Arabia is derived from his membership in the group-family, village and tribe, and is not determined by his individual capacities. The Arab tribesman is, thus, an integral part of his group and has no thought of ever going beyond it. Moreover, the mark of a Bedouin is his complete absorption in tribal life. A man does not affect his tribe, but the tribe does affect the man. The tribe, sub-tribe, and family are the primary objects of personal loyalty. Attachment to the tribe is evident in the consistent Bedouin refusal to imagine living in the different land. As one Arab poet said:

> "My Country, even if it is bitter to me, would still be loved by me, and my family, even if they think badly about me, would still be loved by me."[7]

This verse, in Arabic, would be pronounced as follows:

> Beladi wa'en jarat alaya azizatun, waahli wa'en danu alaya keramo.

The most outstanding characteristics of Bedouin heritage are bravery, hospitality, and generosity. Accordingly, the Bedouin may slaughter his best goat to provide a meal for guests. Arab society, in general, adopted these values centuries ago. Modernization has done little to dilute them at any level, particularly in Saudi society.

Descendents of Bedouins who live in cities and villages (like the royal family, who trace their origins to the Anazah tribe of northern Arabia and parts of Jordan), remain proud of their desert roots.

[7]Author's translation.

An important aspect of the Islamic family relationship is that the child must respect and obey his parents and remain part of the family until he or she marries.[8] The Qur'an teaches that obedience to and respect for one's parents is a sacred duty. Saudis do not need to visit psychiatrists because their culture dictates solving problems through talking and sharing solutions to problems with a grandmother or grandfather, an aunt or uncle, and in many cases, "it works!" Even men in their thirties maintain a subservience to family authority, and reliance on the advice of elders.

In the Arab family, the father holds the child and hugs the baby up to the age of five or six. Beyond that age, the child is more active and becomes closer to the mother than the father. The father often sits in the center of the living room, but the mother never sits very close to him, nor does she hug or kiss him, or hold his hand in front of the children or any member of the family.

Marriage, according to Islam, is the fundamental institution which aims at establishing the family, the first unity of society. Marriage is considered a means of reinforcing extensive group values, including the perpetuation of the extended family. In the United States, marriage means love, sex, procreation, and companionship to the degree of importance determined by the marriage partners. Marriages are easy to come by for Westerners and difficult to come by for Saudis. Divorces are not as fast or easy as they generally are for Westerners.

Saudi customs normally dictate the order in which sons and daughters are permitted to marry. In most cases, the

[8]In some cases, depending on the family's wealth, children stay in the paternal home even after marriage.

parents insist that the oldest son or the oldest daughter be offered in marriage prior to the other children. The oldest son of any family is expected to remain with his parents after marriage. If the son should leave his parents' home, it is considered to be shameful and not in keeping with tradition. Additionally, the son is expected to provide a home for and support his parents in their later years. This practice is in decline, however.

Procreation is traditionally regarded as the true aim of marriage in the Kingdom. On the whole, marriage is a complicated and serious affair in Saudi Arabia. It involves money and the joining of a large number of people, not just two. Therefore, the process of getting married in Saudi Arabia is not an easy one.

Marriage in Saudi Arabia is completely planned. Marriage arrangements are made between the bride's father and the groom's father. Normally, a dowry for the bride is payable to the bride's father before the marrige arrangement is finalized. The amount of the dowry varies depending on tribal affiliation and wealth. Wedding ceremonies are normally performed in the home of the groom, and the male and female guests are completely separated until the actual ceremony is performed. Generally speaking, marriage customs have begun to change slowly during this decade, owing to the influence of Western culture. Saudi men educated abroad sometimes marry girls of their own choice. In the conservative areas of the country, it is common for senior members of Saudi families to marry teenage brides.

It is considered essential that a woman be a virgin before marriage. In fact, a woman's honor is seen as her most

important asset. The honor of the entire family becomes
dependent on maintaining the virginity of sisters and daughters. A man's honor is also reflected in his wife being a
virgin on their wedding night.[9]

Intermarrying is quite common in Saudi Arabia due to
the close family ties, even to the extent that widows of
deceased members of a family are commonly united with
the brother-in-law or cousin. Because of the importance of
tribal affiliations, a woman does not become a member of
her husband's family, nor does she change her name. The
preferred marriage partner for a man, traditionally, is his
father's brother's daughter (cousin).

If a Saudi man or woman plans to be married to a
non-Saudi, they must obtain permission from the Ministry
of the Interior for initial approval and finalize it through the
Ministry of Justice. Moreover, a Saudi man is allowed to
marry a non-Muslim woman who believes in the Judaic-
Christian religions, but a Muslim woman is not permitted to
marry a non-Muslim man.

I was told by an Imam that it is forbidden for a Muslim
woman to marry a man from the people of the book.
However, it is acceptable for a Muslim man to marry a
Christian or a Jew because according to Islam, children
follow their fathers. Customarily, it is the wife who moves
into her husband's home and joins his family; their children
take his name. In this way, the whole family is raised in an
Islamic atmosphere. The reverse happens when a Muslim
woman marries a believer of another religion.[10]

[9]For an interesting description of honor in the Arab world, see: Ralph Patai,
The Arab Mind, (New York: Charles Scribner's Sons), 1973.
[10]The author's source prefers to remain anonymous.

Courtship and dating may differ considerably within countries belonging to the same general culture. In some Arabian countries, such as Egypt, Syria, Lebanon, and Palestine, courtship and dating are easier than in others. The boy has to know the girl, and she must introduce him to her whole family. He must spend time getting acquainted with her parents, then he may ask permission to escort their daughter to the theater or to dinner for several hours. When he brings her home, he must see one of her parents so they know that he brought her, and that she did not walk home by herself. In Saudi Arabia and Kuwait there is no dating. There is no communication between a man and a woman unless they are married or related, or one of them is a shopkeeper or in some occupation involving public contact. The dating in Egypt and other countries with similar customs is designed to culminate in marriage. As noted earlier, marriages in Saudi Arabia are arranged by the bride's father and the groom's father.

At the time of the engagement ceremony, the parents of the boy and girl gather in one of their houses and celebrate the engagement. They exchange presents, and the boy gives the engagement ring to the girl, and vice-versa.

In Arab countries, people have to be invited to the wedding ceremony. Saudi Arabian women go inside the house where the marriage is to be held and meet the bride and bridegroom. The women drink coffee and tea and talk about the wedding; how much it cost, how lucky and beautiful the bride is, and how lucky she is to be getting married. Some of the women who are related to one of the persons getting married dance for this ceremony. This dance is a special one, different than western dances. The invited men, either husbands to the women inside the house or friends of the families, gather outside the house. They gather in the street, which is blocked off, carpeted, and decorated with assorted lights and tents. The people drink tea and coffee and talk. The bridegroom leaves the house to greet and dance with the invited friends. He then goes to his room until the next morning. The men dance throughout the evening. They stand in two parallel lines and start dancing and singing. There are two helpers to the singer who aid in sending the words to the ends of the two lines. They sing and dance in time by taking steps backward and forward until the two lines of people are close enough to touch shoulders.

Saudis are intense in their friendships. For example, should a Saudi meet a friend in the street, he will insist on inviting him to his home, or to a cafe or restaurant if his home is too far away. If while driving his automobile he should see a friend walking in the street, he will stop and insist on giving him a lift, even if the friend is heading in the opposite direction.

In Saudi Arabia, people tend to be social and friendly with peers. They maintain lifelong friendships which carry over into working relationships.

In Arabian countries, male-male friendship permits sitting close together, holding hands when walking, or sharing a meal from the same plate. Male-female friendships are non-existent in most of these countries.

Arabian preservation of ancient learning and their own achievements in mathematics, astronomy, science and medicine were the foundation for these modern disciplines. Arabs taught Europeans to play chess, the guitar, and the tambourine. Many words used in the United States and Europe originated in the Arabic language. For example, cotton, coffee, lemon, and sugar are words of Arabic origin.

Perhaps most importantly, science itself originated in Arab lands. *Aljabar,* meaning algebra, was systemized by Arab mathematicians. Early Arab astronomers provided the concept of the solar calendar, as well as information about star and planet positions, which greated assisted early navigation efforts.

It is worth noting that the Arab's pride in being Arabic is profound. Islam gave the Arabs earthly greatness, and it was the Arabs who gave Islam its earthly success.[11]

Most Arabs adhere to either Islam or Christianity. The majority are Muslims. Muslims gather inside a mosque for their worship. They believe the mosque is the house of God. Mosques are of two general sizes. One is small, holding about fifty to one hundred people; in these the people who live within three or four blocks gather for the daily prayers of Islam, since the second type of mosque, the "grand" mosque, is usually too far away.

On Fridays, all Muslims gather in the nearest grand mosque to pray and listen to a speech from the religious leader, who is called the "Imam." Some people gather after the prayer to discuss and study religion and its effect on their lives. Arabian Christians use the same custom of worship as that practiced by American Christians.

Arabic is spoken by 120 million people. This statistic becomes even more meaningful when expessed in comparative terms. For example, Arabic is more widely spoken than German; it is spoken by forty million more people than is

[11]Wilfred Cantwell Smith, *Islam in Modern Times,* (Princeton, N.J.: Princeton University Press, 1977), p. 160.

French, and by sixty million more people than is Italian.

The tone of Arab conversations is generally loud, although the participants may actually be speaking with little emotion. Often an Arab appears to Westerners to be angry or excited. However, personal status may modulate vocal tone; by lowering his voice and almost mumbling, the Saudi shows respect to his superior. Gestures, facial expressions, and intonation are important aspects of communication.

In the Middle East, if you hear a group of Arabs discussing something, it may sound like they are all shouting angrily at once. Actually, the loudness is a way of emphasizing a point and is not meant to express anger or hostility. This communication pattern is a part of the Arab's culture, and it is important that it not be ignored. If the Arab does not boast and exaggerate, he feels he might be misunderstood. If the Arab does not talk loudly, it may be a sign to others that he means the opposite. The Arab, who is only following a communication tradition of his culture, may easily be misunderstood by the non-Arab who misses the Arab's intent or attaches undue importance to the over-emphasized, assertive, and exaggerated argumentative style of the Arab.

Communication, in some of its most subtle aspects, differs greatly from one country to another. Every culture incorporates concepts of space and time in its communication, and even the way we look at and speak to others is influenced by our cultural pattern. The concepts of one culture may vastly differ from those of another, but if we understand the reasons for these differences, our ability to communicate will be generally enhanced.

Saudis are courteous, which means they agree with you whenever you present something as yours—your idea, your plan, your suggestion. If you ask whether something is good and the person hesitates before he agrees (and even if he continues to agree), the initial hesitation is a strong clue that he might, in reality, disagree. He is just too polite to say it.

In the Middle East, people like to watch others. They even watch the pupils of the eye to judge the responses to different matters. Pupils are very sensitive indicators of how people respond to a situation. When someone says something you do not like, your pupils tend to contract.

Arabs do a lot of touching during a conversation. The touching could be to the wrist, hand, shoulder, or the head. Generally, Arabs breathe on people when they talk. To them, good smells are pleasing and a way of being involved with each other while building relations.

When an Arab meets an American, the Arab is apt to take offense when the American stands back at the customary American distance, i.e.; 'the four-to-seven foot social consultative distance.' The Arab complains that Americans do not care about other people. Once, an Arabian was admitted to an American hospital for surgery—he felt that he was ignored; that his nurse was not taking good care of him because she stayed so far away. Another Arabian in a similar situation remarked in response to this American behavior, "What is the matter? Do I smell bad?"

In formal Arab-American communication, difficulties may arise due to cultural differences about the use of space. Once, a newly-arrived American diplomat was carrying on a conversation with his Arab host. As was the custom in the Arabian country, the Arab moved up very close to the

American. This made the American uncomfortable, so he
retreated a few feet. Not accustomed to such a distance, the
Arab moved again, and again the American retreated. The
comedy of advance and retreat continued until the Arab had
literally chased the American across the width of the room.
The American impression of the Arab was that he was
pushy, whereas the Arab regarded the American as cold and
aloof.

In a social conversation, or in opening business conversation, there is a give-and-take of good-humored small talk
centering on the health and well-being of the other party.
Meetings for any purpose are rarely convened punctually,
and are apt to drag on.

Time and schedules operate differently in Saudi Arabia.
Patience is not only considered a virtue in the Kingdom, it is
an entire way of life.[12] In other words, Saudis are on cordial
terms with time, and the thought of "killing" it has never
crossed their minds. Moreover, elaborate rituals of hospitality are still required to set the stage for serious talk. Deci-
sions cannot be made under the pressure of time. "Yes" and
"no" answers are avoided if at all possible, but infinite
variations of "maybe" are available.[13]

In the Middle East, some male adults arrive home whenever they please. Children, however, are supposed to be
home before their father arrives. In the United States,
people are more aware of time. If the husband is going to be
late getting home, he usually calls to let his wife know of his

---

[12]If I am allowed to confirm this by my personal experience, I would say that it is
in observing the Saudis I was able to establish this fact.

[13]William B. Quandt, *Saudi Arabia in the 1980's: Foreign Policy and Oil,* (Washington, D.C.: The Brooking Institution), p. 150.

delay. If someone telephones very early in the morning, or after midnight, it usually signals a serious matter.

An Arabian businessman once invited an American to his house by requesting, "Won't you and your family come and visit us? Come any time, please." After many weeks the Arabian repeated the invitation. The American answered that he would like to drop in, but never did. To an American, "Come any time," is just an expression of friendliness; unless a time is specified, the invitation is not to be taken seriously. In the Middle East, the words are meant literally—the host is putting himself at the disposal of his guest and really expects him to visit. If the guest never visits, the host assumes that he does not want to come.

In the office setting, it is pointless to make an appointment far ahead of time, because the informal structure of the Arabian time system places everything beyond one week ahead into a single category of "future." Any period longer than a week is generally too indefinite to consider.

Tardiness and slowness are acceptable in Arabian countries. It is thought that if you aren't willing to take the time to sit down and have coffee with people, you have a problem. You must learn to wait, and not be too eager to talk business. Two American businessmen once went to an Arabian country to discuss business with a firm. They spent almost two full days with no results, but during the last two hours at the hotel, they signed their contract.

In the Middle East, a person might take his car into a garage and tell the mechanic what is wrong with it. The person might leave the garage, walk around several blocks, and then return to ask the mechanic if he has started working on his car. On his way home for lunch, he might drop by again to ask how things are going. After work he might return again, and see the mechanic working on someone else's car!

Greetings often express an openness or a desire to enter into a conversation. They take many forms and have been given several names by communication theorists, such as small talk. Greetings vary from one culture to another, expressed in phrases such as, "How are you," etc.

In the Middle East, upon greeting, the son and the daughter kiss the hand of their father or mother. This does not happen daily, but only on certain occasions, such as the festival days, or when the father leaves for a long trip. When a person meets a relative he has not seen for a long time, he shouts joyfully, comes toward him, and hugs and kisses him on his cheeks. If that relative is an older man, the person will kiss the man's right hand or right shoulder. This is especially the case if the older man is the father or a very close relative of the person. After kissing, he shakes the right hand for a few minutes, and accompanies this with words of welcome. They talk only about the newcomer's arrival, his health, and how he is doing. This welcome usually lasts for twenty minutes or more.

In the Middle East, if a male visitor comes to an Arabian home, he will be entertained only in the living room. If he needs to use the toilet, he will ask to do so first. The host will then go to be sure it is not occupied, and that everything is in order. The visitor will be escorted by the host to the toilet door. If one family visits another family, the men sit in the living room, and the women sit elsewhere in the house; either in the kitchen or in the hostess' room. It is usual in the Middle East for two men to have known each other well for a number of years without either of them having met the female members of the other's family. This occurs in most Arabian countries. The son serves the tea and coffee to the men. If there is no son, the host will serve the guests. Visitors in Arabian cultures who are friends of the family or relatives are welcome to stay days and nights. It is not necessary or customary to bring or buy food, because guests are not expected to contribute toward any of the expense involved with the visit.

Social parties in the Middle East differ; they depend upon the country's customs and traditions. In Egypt or Palestine, for example, both men and women are invited. They are welcomed by the host and hostess at the door of the house. The male guest shakes hands with the hostess and hugs the host. The female guest kisses the hostess and shakes hands with the host.

In Saudi Arabia and similar countries, social parties are of two kinds. One type is strictly limited to men. The men gather in one house, and hug or shake hands with the host at the door. The other kind of party consists of all women, and no man is welcome.

Everyone in the human race has a name which serves as an identification to which that person can respond.

In the Arab world, if a person wants to talk to another person in the street and does not know who he is, he will address him, "Hey, man." If he knows the person but not very well, he will call him by his first name, such as "Abdulla." If he knows that person very well, knows that he has children, and that his eldest child is a son named, perhaps, "Adel," he will then call him by his first son's name, adding the prefix "Abu," which means "father of," i.e., "Abu Adel."

If the person addressed has a daughter but no son, and the daughter's name is, for example, "Nawal," it is up to him whether he wishes to be called by his daughter's name. If so, he will be called "Abu Nawal." If not, he will be called by his nickname.

Similarly, a woman is given a *kunya* (nickname) by combining the prefix "Umm," meaning "mother of," with a child's name.

Here are some names and nicknames for men and women.

Names for Men	Nicknames for Men
Ibrahim	Abu Khalil
Abdulla	Abu Mohammad
Mohammad	Abu Jassim
Khalid	Abu Waleed

Names for Women	Nicknames for Women
Mariam	Umm Eisa
Fatima	Umm Kassem
Nora	Umm Adel
Haleema	Umm Sa'ad

In the Arabian world, when people are not known, they are addressed with a title of respect, such as "Hadji," "Imam," or "Sidi." Some people are addressed as Syid, Ustadh, Shaikh, etc., the particular name depending upon the position the person holds. Hadji, Imam, Sidi, and Shaikh are titles of respect given to religious men. Shaikh is also used for those holding government positions, or for quite wealthy people.

Syid is a title for any respected person, whether we know him or not. Ustadh usually is a title of respect for educated persons, teachers and writers. There are also specific titles for military personnel, such as general, captain, sergeant, etc.

The following observations may further help the reader to better understand what is acceptable, unacceptable or expected within Saudi society.

— Saudis traditionally have considered the left hand "unclean," for it is the hand that is supposed to be used for performing toilet functions. To point it at someone or to gesture with it may still be considered insulting in the more traditional areas of the country. Similarly, it has been considered offensive to eat with the left hand.

— Wise-cracking and barnyard humor, which are acceptable at certain times and places in the United States and Western Europe, are generally inappropriate in Saudi Arabia.

— Part of the Saudi culture is the practice of bargaining over prices. It is not insulting to the shopkeepers and in fact it is expected. Modern stores are moving away from bargaining and are going to fixed prices with occasional sales, as in Western cultures.

— It is not unusual to see Saudis demonstrate a great amount of affection between members of the same sex; but such demonstrations are almost never seen between members of the opposite sex.

— There still remains the traditional restriction of freedom of movement for women. Social life is segregated by sexes. Saudi women are indistinguishable and unapproachable.

— Saudis use "Shaikh" as a title for religious leaders, an acknowledgement of respect for public figures, and it traditionally applies to the leader of a tribe.

— It is a common practice within families in the Kingdom for men to give gifts of gold to women.

— There is little variation in general life style, dress or religion. Most Saudi men still wear the traditional Arab *thobe* (*dishadasha*).[14] Saudis wear a red and white head-dress called *ghutra*, sometimes changing to a plain white cloth. The *ghutra* is held in place by an *iqual*, a double ring of black cord. It is often covered by a *mishlah,* or *bisht*, a flowing floor length cloak of light wool. These, along with sandals, are comfortable dress for desert sun and heat.

— Saudi men who wear Western clothes at work some-times modify their dress and actions in the presence of their elders, or on special occasions. Furthermore, long before Islam, men and women in the Middle East knew that it was wise to cover their bodies completely to avoid the disastrous effects of the relentless sun.

— Women in the larger towns wear Western fashions. However, when out-of-doors and outside the imme-diate family circle, they wear an outer garment called an *abayah*. This black, floor-length cloak is worn with a face-covering veil.

— Feeding and food offerings are signs of respect and hospitality. Hospitality is the general custom that a Saudi is expected to practice throughout his life. The Arabs say "a guest is God's gift." Therefore, the guest is always treated as a very distinguished person, no matter

---

[14]"Dishdasha:" The Kuwaiti name for the full-length, shirt-like garment known in the Kingdom as the "thobe." The neckline is round and slit vertically in the center front. It is the ideal garment for all people at all times—comfortable and flattering on all figures.

what his actual position is outside the home. Even in poorer homes, a tremendous effort is made to accommodate a guest.

— Traditionally, each Monday, Saudis as well as other residents of the Kingdom have the opportunity to meet with the King in the *Majlis*[15] regarding their own problems. These people present a written complaint, and the King listens carefully to each individual problem, then refers them to the proper government agency. This enables the authorities to evaluate the matters seriously and to ensure that justice prevails.

— The Saudis greet others by saying *Salam,* the traditional Arabian greeting meaning "Peace be on you." The reply to this is *Wa alaykum al salam*, which means "and upon you be peace."

— The serving of tea or coffee is a common social function that can occur virtually anywhere. It has been suggested that it is polite to drink at least two cups of coffee or tea, but not more than three. To signal that he has had enough, the guest shakes the cup from side to side when handing it back to the coffee server, or he covers the cup with his hand.

— The Saudis main dish is called *kabsa,* which consists of tomato sauce, rice and lamb.

— Frequent visits between women of different households are customary.

— Quarreling between mothers-in-law and daughters-in-law is common.

[15] Saudi Arabians have the right of direct petition to the monarch. The "Majlis" is something like a government forum that is located in a large hall, where the King sits surrounded by his bodyguards, and people gather as they might in an American town hall.

— There are special occasions in the individual's life when an extraordinary show of hospitality is required. Such occasions include marriage, burial, childbirth,[16] finishing the building of a house, and the holy month of Ramadan.

— Neither Saudi nor non-Saudi women are allowed to drive an automobile in the Kingdom, and there are no public cinemas. However, one can very easily live inside Aramco's Dhahran township and never realize one is in the Kingdom. There is a cinema beside the hamburger stand, and women are allowed to drive cars inside the compound.[17]

— Saudis have a high opinion of their values and a deep reverence for their language. They also prize eloquence to a degree perhaps unmatched in any other culture. They are a proud and sensitive people, and their Islam is interwoven with their pride and sensitivity.

— The Saudi approach to life is so intensely personal that every occasion seems to be in a category of its own. From one day to the next, the goal is not to get the job done, or even to acquire a fortune, but rather, to win prestige in other men's eyes and achieve fame tantamount to a state of grace.

— A driver who is involved in a traffic accident must cooperate with local police and furnish a description of the circumstances surrounding the accident, and he

[16]Childbirth is celebrated by food and a male gathering. Male children are an object of pride. It should be noted, however, that the Arab people prefer boys because a girl's life is difficult.

[17]It is understandable why Americans have made themselves at home in Dhahran. More importantly, there are many young men and women who were born, grew up, and are raising children of their own in the company town.

must stay at the scene. Realistically, the chief threat to an individual's safety in the Kingdom is the reckless fatalism exhibited in driving habits. Defensive driving is a must for all, and extreme caution is required when driving on main roads at night.

— Falconry is an ancient winter sport of the Arabian desert, and is actively engaged in by hunters. When the hood is removed from a trained falcon, the bird takes flight in pursuit of its quarry.

— Soccer is the most popular sport in the Kingdom of Saudi Arabia. Scouting and youth clubs are encouraged and supported by the government.

The most important point is that learning about other people's cultures can aid in our understanding and communication, helping up to minimize conflicts. It is also important to note that within the Arab world there are significant differences between various societies, though they do have much in common.

2. Basic Islamic Law in the Kingdom

The following are guidelines regarding unacceptable practices in Saudi Arabia. They apply to foreigners as well as to Saudi citizens.

— No one may bring contraband into Saudi Arabia. Upon arrival at any of the three Saudi international airports (King Khalid International Airport in Riyadh, King Abdul Aziz in Jeddah, or Dhahran International Airport), the traveler must open all his suitcases for a close examination by Customs personnel.

— The law in the Kingdom strictly forbids the importa-
tion, obtainment, possession, or use of items listed
below:[18]

ALCOHOLIC BEVERAGES
WEAPONS, including firearms and knives
NARCOTICS
PORK AND PORK PRODUCTS
PORNOGRAPHY, EROTIC LITERATURE
ANTI-ISLAMIC LITERATURE
ANTI-SAUDI LITERATURE

— Walkie-talkies, citizen's band radios, other transmit-
ting radios, and short-wave radios which receive single
side band signals are also prohibited.

— All alcoholic beverages, their use, distillation or sale,
are forbidden. The penalties for being caught with
alcoholic beverages are severe, and in the case of foreigners, automatically include expulsion from the country with the possibility of a prison sentence preceding
this expulsion.

— Narcotics, except for medicinal purposes, are also not
permitted. Any drugs brought into the Kingdom must
be accompanied by a copy of the prescription and/or a
letter from the prescribing doctor indicating that these
drugs were prescribed for health reasons.

— Do not distribute or display the Bible, crosses, Stars of
David, or religious literature. Do not attempt to import
large quantities of these items.[19]

[18]This prohibition includes importing the materials to construct or fabricate
them.
[19]There is a possibility that Christmas decorations will be confiscated.

— Do not photograph airports, seaports, military or governmental installations without official permission.

— Do not engage in discussions about Saudi politics and government except with close friends. There are other ways, different from Western methods, by which Saudis let their opinions be known to the government.

— Do not insult, curse, or hit a Saudi; you will be sent to jail as a result. In working and living with another culture there is always a potential for misunderstanding and hostility. If you have a short temper, learn to walk away. There is one exception to this rule. If you are a woman and are physically accosted on the street, you have the prerogative of creating a scene, and thus getting other Saudis to intercede for you or to call the police.

— Do not interfere with Saudis observing a religious custom. Do not enter a mosque; non-Muslims are not permitted. Do not walk across a designated prayer area with your shoes on. Do not interrupt or walk in front of a Muslim in prayer, or attempt to buy something or loiter about the shops during prayer times. Do not discuss your opinions on religion.

— Do not interfere with Saudi fasting during Ramadan. It is totally inappropriate to eat, drink, smoke, whistle, sing or play music in front of a Saudi who is fasting, either in public or private.

— Do not interfere with the Saudi social system. Respect of individuals of a higher social status is imperative. Do not contradict these individuals. Do not criticize or overly compliment any Saudi in front of his peers. If you are in a position of authority, expect to be approached to do favors for others. Be as diplomatic as possible and do not accept bribes.

— Never inquire about a Saudi's wife, sister, or daughter. It is not polite to initiate a conversation about these family members. For example, the American question, "How is your wife?" is not appropriate. However, if a Saudi makes a comment about his family members, feel free, at that particular moment, to respond.

— Visiting Saudi homes between the hours of 2 p.m. and 4 p.m. is not recommended. This is the traditional afternoon rest period for most Saudis.

— Do not get involved in financial entanglements. Do not attempt to bribe a Saudi, or buy your way into a situation, agreement, or deal. There is an active system of reciprocity in Saudi Arabia, and you may not be able to meet later demands.

— Do not drive without a license and do not ignore the traffic regulations. You are expected to know and abide by the traffic laws in Saudi Arabia.[20] If you are a woman, you are not permitted to drive, nor are you allowed to take a taxi by yourself. Generally, a woman should not be in public without an escort.

— It is important to note that the holy cities of Makkah and Medina are forbidden to non-Muslims. The third holy place for Muslims is the city of Jerusalem (*AlQuds*),[21]

---

[20] A driver who is involved in a traffic accident must cooperate with local police and furnish a description of the circumstances surrounding the scene of the accident, and he must stay at the scene.

[21] There is no denying that Jerusalem is sacred to the followers of all the three monotheistic religions: Judaism, Christianity and Islam. Therefore, Jerusalem is universal in its religious significance. "AlQuds" means Jerusalem in Arabic.

where the Alaqsa Mosque is located. Significantly, the journey by night of the Prophet Muhammad from Haram Mosque in Jerusalem is called *Isr'a*, and the *Mi'raq* is the ascent of the Prophet from Alaqsa to heaven to meet Allah. It was on this occasion that Prophet Muhammad received orders from Allah to introduce the Muslim practice of praying five times daily.

Saudi Arabia interprets its laws very strictly, but the religious judges tend to be just and humane in their case-by-case interpretations of the Islamic law (*Shari'ah*). In theory, the "Shari'ah" provides guidance for every aspect of the life of every individual and of the community, which of course includes the state.

Therefore, Shari'ah courts exercise jurisdiction in all spheres of life (civil, criminal, and family).

Basically, Islamic law distinguishes between the right of God (Allah) and the rights of man. Punishment is only specified for crimes against Allah. These crimes include adultery, false accusation of adultery, drinking alcohol, theft, robbery, murder, hostility and war against Muslims, attempting to overthrow the Islamic order, and high treason. The punishments for crimes against Allah are called *hadd*, and include death (by sword, stoning, or crucifixion), or flogging (up to one hundred lashes). Abortion is considered a crime unless it is necessary to protect the life of the mother. As in Western law, ignorance is no excuse.

In order to confirm an adultery charge, the Shari'ah requires a minimum of three Muslim witnesses to the actual intercourse act itself, or a repeated confession. It is of interest that a female is only counted as half a witness. If both the man and woman admit to the act of their own free will, they will receive as their sentence death by stoning. However, the testimony of a non-Muslim will not be accepted.

Those who have committed murder may be imprisoned until the victim's eldest son reaches maturity and is able to decide between the alternatives of blood-money or execution. If execution is chosen, the killer is beheaded in a public square on a Friday. Thieves have their right hand amputated.

In the analysis of the author, the severity of punishment serves to deter crime, and reinforces the desire of individuals to live within the limits of the law. This in turn protects the majority from those who might otherwise commit crimes.

Of importance to those who live and work in Saudi Arabia, the country enjoys a high degree of security and a lower crime rate than that of many other countries. Armed robberies and other forms of violent crime continue to be almost unknown in the Kingdom of Saudi Arabia.

It is important to point out that the ideology of the Islamic state is nothing but the thought that real sovereignty and lordship belong only to God, and that it is his law which lays down the rules of human conduct. Hence, the obligation of the Islamic state to establish its juridicial, educational and administrative policies on the basis of protecting and strengthening family life.

The state alone can be in charge of punishment. Individuals or families should not attempt this on their own. Hence, the Islamic state cannot be run without its government being fully committed to Islam.[22]

[22]Hamid Enayat, *Modern Islamic Political Thought,* (Austin: University of Texas Press, 1982), p. 107.

3. The Role of Islam in Saudi Life

The following discussion is an analysis of the role of Islam in Saudi society.

(1) Islam affirms the absolute unity of God. The Islamic tradition was formed on the principle that destiny is in the hands of God. There is a firm belief that God has ordained all action, and that man cannot alter the course of events that God sets. Allah is the proper Arabic name for God, and it is Allah who controls events. Saudis know that Allah gave them all the wealth that they enjoy, and so they feel neither lucky nor surprised about their good fortune, and they are grateful to no one excpet Allah and themselves. To the Saudis, of course, Islam is the religion of God.

The Arab Muslim is, like other Muslims, proud of his faith. No other religion in the world has been as successful as Islam in eliciting a confessional pride in its adherents. In the Arab case this pride in Islam is not separate from his national enthusiasm, but infuses it and gives it strength.

As dawn breaks over the sea, the desert, and the imposing buildings of modern Saudi Arabia, the *muezzin* (announcer of the call to prayer) climbs the minaret and summons the faithful to prayer with these words:[23]

[23]For anyone who has visited a Muslim country, the two opening phrases, "Allaho Akbar" (which means, "Allah is great,"), and "Ash-hadu an la illah illa Allah, Mohammad Rasoul Allah," will linger in the mind.

> *Haya ala al-salat*
> *Haya ala al-falah*
> *Al-salat khayran min al-noum*
> *Allaho akbar*
> *Ash-hadu an la illah illa allah*

Allah is most great.
I testify that
There is no god but Allah
and that Muhammad
is the Prophet of Allah.
Come to the Prayer!

Come to Salvation!
Prayer is better than sleep.
Allah is most great
There is no god but Allah.

The call to prayer is made five times a day. Only the dawn prayer includes the phrase, "Prayer is better than sleep." Each phrase is repeated twice.

As a public place of worship for Muslims, the mosque has a special importance. These places of worship are often historically valuable, architectually striking and esthetically beautiful.

From Malaysia to Morocco, the typical mosque has the same basic form. Exteriors are often rectangular in outline, with interiors consisting of a central, open court surrounded by a cloister or walkway covered by a roof on top of rows of pillars. A dome often covers the mosque's central court. The wall facing the Ka'ba in Mecca contains a prayer niche or *Mahrab* towards which worshippers face when they pray. Rising above most mosques—vertical extensions of them—are one or more minarets from which *muezzins* call the faithful to prayer five times a day. Most mosques have three features in common; fountains or faucets used by Muslims to wash before prayer, space for worshippers to pray, and a pulpit, or *minbar,* from which a learned member of the Muslim community gives the Friday sermon.

(2) Saudi behavior is motivated by Islamic values. For example, the term *Insha Allah* is used to express the following meanings:

a. If God wills it.

b. Keep trying.

c. If possible, or if all goes well.

d. Yes, but with an escape clause.

In fact, the expression "if God wills it (Insha Allah)", is the answer to every question you can ask Saudis about the future. Such a response clearly indicates the vast difference between Saudis and Western practices.

(3) The verse *Ma Sha Allah* means Allah has willed it. Significantly, God is present in the Saudi consciousness at most times, and everyday events or activities are believed to be determined by Allah's will. It is no surprise then, that when a Saudi is asked about his work, his health, or his family, he will reply with a basic philosophy of Muslim life; *alhamdoolilah,* which means, "All thanks and praise to Allah."

(4) Traditionally, Saudis are supposed to begin all acts with the name of Allah. The phrase *Basmallah,* which means "In the name of Allah, the Compassionate, the Merciful," is spoken before undertaking almost any activity; eating, giving a speech, reciting the Holy Qur'an, opening a shop, starting a vehicle, etc. Saudis believe that any activity not begun with these words is severed from its blessing. (See Appendix 3.)

(5) The most outstanding characteristic of the average Saudi is his fundamentally religious outlook on life.

In Saudi Arabia, the ethical behavior of the individual, as prescribed in the Qur'an, applies to the entire community.

It is the reponsibility of the state, as organizer of the community, to promote and facilitate such behavior. For example, in Saudi Arabia, radio and television are interrupted for prayer time, and all businesses are closed by law during this period; this is enforced by the religious police.[24] Common values tend to legitimate existing social relations and to stabilize them, thus contributing to the maintenance of social order. Precisely, human behavior is a function of the culture; as culture varies, so will behavior.[25]

(6) Women and their behavior are specifically mentioned in the Holy Qur'an. The Saudi women today take their behavior from these writings. In the Holy Qur'an it is written: "Say to the believing women, do not give daring looks, cover the body, do not show your beauty, unless, like the eyes, it is already revealed." It was not until 1926 that the veiling of women was made legally compulsory in Saudi Arabia. While non-Saudi women do not have to be veiled in the Kingdom, they should not wear tight-fitting sweaters or clothing, shorts, very short skirts or sleeveless tops in public. Therefore, long-sleeved dresses or long-sleeved blouses are essential for women during trips to town or public places. Men should avoid shorts or "cut-offs." In Islam, men must wear clothes that cover the parts of their body between the navel and the knee. In addition, a man cannot wear silk or gold, according to Islam.

(7) The Islamic faith grants a man the privilege of having four wives at any given time. But he must give wives

---

[24]Prayer (salat) is performed five times a day; at dawn (fajar), noon (duhr), afternoon (assr), sunset (maghreb), and night (isha'h).

[25]Gloria B. Levitas, Culture and Consciousness, (New York: George Braziller, Inc., 1967), p. 137.

number two, three, and four exactly what he has given to number one. The Qur'an places a man under the obligation to treat all his wives in a similar manner with equal kindness and fairness. To quote the Qur'an: "If you feel you cannot be quite fair to all your wives, take one."[26]

I was told by an Imam[27] that marriage is urged on Muslims as necessary for the perpetuation of vital manpower. This thinking is apparent in the permission given to men to have more than one wife.

Women are traditionally dressed with their bodies draped from head to toe in shapeless black shrouds.[28]. With their opaque, black veils always completely hiding their faces, they are indistinguishable and unapproachable. Above the age of nine, the only men that women are permitted to meet unveiled are husbands and close relations. The veil is still one of the most fascinating mysteries in the Kingdom.

Women's clothes must cover the entire body except the face and hands. Moreover, a woman's clothes must be loose so as not to expose the shape of her body. According to Islam, a woman's body is not for public display. In some countries, clothing for women is designed with sexual motives.[29]

[26] Author's translation.

[27] Literally, he who leads his fellow Muslims in prayer at Saudi Mosque facing "Al-Ka'aba." "Al-Ka'aba" is the small building inside the Great Mosque at Mecca which contains the sacred black stone. Al-Ka'aba is considered by Muslims to be the house of Allah built by Patriarch Ibrahim and his son Ishmael. During the 3,000 years since its original conception, it has been destroyed several times as a result of war or natural disaster. Each time it was built on the same site, because of its unique significance.

[28] This is referred to as the "Lawful Dress," which in Arabic is called "Al-Ziyy Al-Shari."

[29] Mohammad Ali Alkhuli, *The Light of Islam,* (Riyadh: Saudi Arabia, 1981), p. 93.

(8) Segregation of the sexes is practiced by Saudis. This longstanding tradition is even present in Saudi architecture. Saudi houses still have separate entrances and separate reception rooms for men and women.

In Saudi society, the men and women do not entertain together. Social life is segregated by sexes. Men have their circle of male friends and women have their circle of female friends. Public affairs are also segregated, with certain times and places for men and women. Buses are partitioned by a gate. Females occupy the back section of the bus, and males occupy the front section.

Female students cannot be taught by male instructors in the Western face-to-face classroom method. All schools are segregated by sex. A shortage of female teachers hampers education in some respects. For example, if there are no female teachers for a certain subject, instruction by a male teacher must be accomplished by using booths equipped with earphones or projection screens, or the male instructor must be blind.

A female's life is not like a male's. In Saudi Arabia, a woman's main purpose in life is to marry and have children. A woman is totally dependent on her husband. However, in Saudi Arabia there are jobs that women may perform outside the home, and many educated Saudi women are working in the field of education as teachers and counselors. Traditional Bedouin women, on the other hand, care for the children, cook, weave, and embroider, pitch and load their tents, and gather fuel.

Contrary to widespread belief in the West, nothing exists in the Holy Qur'an to suggest that Muslim women do not have the same religious rights and duties as men, or that women should be kept ignorant and uneducated. But conventional attitudes in the West still view Islam as a negative social and political philosophy.

In Saudi Arabia, the adult Arab male dominates. Women, wives, and children are obliged to submit to his authority. The female members of a family usually walk five paces behind the males. Moreover, men and women do not converse with one another outside the home.

It is true that a woman's share of property is less than that of the man's, and the Qur'an states, "Men are a degree above them."[30] This specifies that man is the head of the household, something which has been practiced and rarely disputed in most societies until the days of women's liberation movements.[31] Furthermore, a Saudi man can divorce any of his wives relatively simply, but not without assuming certain obligations, such as provisions for the children. Generally, but not always, the man receives the custody of all male children over seven and females over the age of twelve.

A Saudi Imam told me that whatever the interpretation of the social relations, with the exception of a few individuals, the West is beginning to act either indifferently or even in opposition to Muslims.[32] The status of women under Islam is probably one of the least understood subjects in the non-Muslim world today. Traditionally it has been a system of social spheres in which men and women have had

[30] Author's translation.

[31] For nearly fourteen centuries, Muslim women have had independent property rights that have been denied to women in most Western countries until recently.

[32] Author's translation of the statement by an Imam from Dammam, Saudi Arabia, on August 20, 1983.

specific roles to play—the women's role centering around marriage, the children, and the home, where they reigned supreme, and the men's role centering around business and public affairs.

(9) The study of the Qur'an is considered to be the most valuable of academic studies among conservative Saudis. Contests are held and prizes awarded to the contestant who can best recite the Holy Qur'an from memory. Most importantly, the Saudis are religious in the sense of unquestioning belief in their traditions and obedience to the religious rituals which have circumscribed their lives.

Islam for Saudis is not an abstract idea but an idea put into practice. The Qur'an is regarded as presenting a perfect pattern to be applied, rather than an imperative to seek perfection.[33] Saudis believe that man is the summit of creation, and that God has not left mankind without guidance. He sent Adam as the first prophet to guide human beings, and Muhammad as the last prophet. The combined social, ideological, religious, and legal impact of Islam in Saudi Arabia gives religious leaders considerable influence in the Kindgom.

(10) One important aspect of the Hajj is that it provides the pilgrim with the opportunity to take a new name. When talking to someone who has returned from the pilgrimage, it is necessary to address that person as "Hajj," before saying his first name (as in "Hajj Abdullah"). It is considered to be insulting to omit the title "Hajj," because this is interpreted as minimizing the great significance of pilgrimage.

[33]Edward Said and Fuad Suleiman, The Arabs Today: Alternatives for Tomorrow, (Columbus, Ohio: Forum Associates, 1973), p. 290.

The singleness of belief in an omnipotent God who is Almighty and remote is illustrated in a Muslim saying which may be translated as follows:

"Whatever concept your mind comes to, I tell you flatly, Allah is not that." (*Kul Ma Khatar be balik faho halek wallaho ghair tha lek.*)

This concept is, of course, very far from the Christian idea that God made himself known in human flesh to human beings. No Muslim would think of calling God a "father" because a father is a purely human concept.

As a dynamic religious and cultural movement, Islam encourages its followers to seek knowledge in all forms and from all sources. Indeed, the Saudi leadership believes that the Islamic teachings incorporate virtually every aspect of life, whatever its content, and they also maintain the view that it is the Islamic patterns of behavior which give Saudi society its cohesion as well as its vitality.

As we have seen, Islam is not only a set of religious beliefs and devotions. It also provides rules and guidance for behavior in private, social, and business life. Islam is central to every aspect of Saudi society.

To Saudis, Islam means dignity, equality, social justice, culture and civilization. Islam is also credited with saving the Arabic language from degeneration.

The Qur'an states, "Had your Lord willed, He could indeed have made mankind one nation, yet they will not cease to differ."[34] This verse reflects the Islamic belief that cultural differences will always exist in the world, and that this is as it should be.

[34] *Qur'an II, Verse 118.*

It is important to respect these differences, and to view Islam as an alternative, in addition to Judiasm and Christianity, and significantly, as neither East nor West.[35]

[35] Saudi society does not operate by Western logic. Islam, like Judaism, provides a complete system of social legislation based on divine sanctions. Islam comes nearer to Judaism than to Christianity. On the other hand, like Christianity, it delivers a universal message.

PART THREE

DEVELOPMENT AND MODERNIZATION

1. Overview

Saudi Arabia's oil began to flow to the international market in the early 1940's. The revenues from this created the opportunity for economic and social development. This brought about some degree of improvement in the general standard of living, which had fallen to a desperate level.

Since then, the national economy has depended almost totally on oil revenues as a source of income. The wealth derived from oil is temporary and transitory; it only assumes real economic significance if used to create alternative sources of income for long-term economic gain, rather than short-term commercial exchange.

Oil was discovered in 1936.[1] The first tanker load of Saudi oil left Ras Tanura in May, 1939, but actual large-scale production did not begin until 1945.

The Kingdom is the world's largest oil exporter, and ranks with the United States and the Soviet Union as one of the three largest oil producers.

Saudi Arabia has some fifty oil fields. The Ghawar field is 150 miles long and 25 miles across at its greatest width; it is the largest oil field in the world. Safaniya, in the Arabian Gulf, is the world's largest off-shore oil operation. Ras Tanura and Ju'aymah are the biggest and busiest oil terminals in the world.[2]

[1]Oil was first struck in December, 1936, at a well called Dammam No. 7.
[2]Oil production levels are set by political, technical, and economic considerations.

The country's total recoverable oil reserves, about 168 billion barrels, are the largest of any country in the world. This represents more than six times the size of U.S. reserves.

Generally, people know that Saudi Arabia is rich in oil. However, few know that precious metals are also plentiful. By the 1990's, the Kingdom is expected to produce an estimated thirty tons of gold and ninety tons of silver, as well as measurable quantities of copper and zinc.

Saudi wealth and consequent political influence are derived from (a) the revenue generated by oil production and (b) the industrial West's ability to provide goods and services, safe investment opportunities, and the means for development.[3]

Saudi Arabia's crucial role in world energy affairs, with an estimated one-quarter of the world's oil reserves under its land, needs no emphasis.

The declared policy of the Kingdom is to develop a viable economy based on refined petroleum products. The scale and speed of Saudi development has raised economic and political questions of worldwide significance. The consequences of these developments are far-reaching in time and scope, requiring careful planning in order to steer a clear course in the decades ahead.[4]

Industrialization depends on certain fundamental factors. Saudi Arabia is committed to industrialization as the key to building a strong, diversified economy. The extent to which these factors are present or absent is clearly a major

[3]Quandt, *Op. Cit.*, pp. 170-180.
[4]His Excellency Sheikh Hisham Nazir, the Planning Minister, a very well-known and educated doctor, has played an important role in the country's development.

issue in the overall economic strategy. The factors can be summarized as follows:

— Raw material and primary products
— Market
— Infrastructure
— Manpower and technical skills
— Revenues
— Government support

It is important to note that the Master Gas System (MGS) is a major element in Saudi Arabia's ambitious industrialization program.

An industrialization process that took a century or more in Western Europe is being carried out in Saudi Arabia in only a fraction of that time span. This industrialization is, naturally, based on oil and gas production. The MGS insures that these finite resources are utilized to the fullest to achieve the successful completion of the Kingdom's development plans.

Saudi Arabia's third Five-Year Economic Development Plan (1980-1985), has as its major goals the improvement of the standard of living of all the Kingdom's citizens, the full utilization of the infrastructure created during the first two plans to diversify the productive base, an increase in the productivity of Saudi manpower through improved educational and training facilities (with an attendant decline in dependence on expatriate labor), the containment of inflation, and the streamlining of the government's administrative machinery.

How the standard of living of Saudi citizens will be improved can be seen from this partial list of Plan targets:

— huge boosts in urban water supply, with fifty percent of the population to have potable water within easy reach.

— large tracts of land to be brought under irrigation or to undergo conversion from traditional to modern irrigation methods.

— substantially increased loans to the agricultural sector to improve seed quality, poultry and dairy processing, and animal health.

— Eighty percent of the population to have access to utility-supplied electric power, with generating capacity to increase by about 7,500 mw to 12,400 mw; 6,300 kilometers of transmission and sub-transmission lines to be commissioned.

— five new cement plants planned, including two joint ventures with Bahrain and Kuwait, with a total capacity of 23,000 tons a day; existing plants to increase capacity by 13,400 tons a day.

— total of some SR 440 billion to be invested in the private sector, government ministries and defense.

— twenty-five new main road programs to add 4,400 kilometers to the system.

— port expansion to allow a fifty percent increase in imports.

— new international airports at Jeddah and Riyadh, three domestic airports to be built at Tayif, Hofuf and Baha.

— approximately 800 kilometers of railroad track to be constructed or replaced.

— more than 250,000 housing units to be built by the public and private sectors.

Dr. Abdulhadi Tahr, Governor of the General Petroleum and Mineral Organization (Petromin), has outlined the

Kingdom's national objectives for energy development in his book, *Energy: A Global Outlook.*[5] These objectives include:

— development of an integrated national oil and gas enterprise with special emphasis on development of a national marketing capability to serve international oil and gas markets.
— increased processing of petroleum in Saudi Arabia.
— increased national participation in the international energy transportation industry.
— augmentation of current oil and gas reserves and production capacities.
— development of alternative sources of energy.
— international cooperation with special emphasis on promoting developing countries' interests in the field of energy.

The Petromin Governor has clearly indicated the importance of the MGS to the fullfillment of the Kingdom's energy goals: "The Master Gas System for the gathering, treating and transmission of associated gas, previously flared, is destined to stand as a milestone in the development of the international gas industry."[6]

Not only will the MGS produce a net addition to the availability of hydrocarbon derivatives in the world market, it will also allow for the substitution of gas for oil in the water desalination and power generating plants. Furthermore, underground storage of NGL (Natural Gas Liquifi-

[5]Abdulhadi Tahr, *Energy: A Global Outlook,* (Saudi Arabia: Government Printing Office, 1981).
[6]*Main Gas System* (Houston, Texas: Aramco, 1981).

cation) products will serve as a signficant step towards conservation and the development of national energy reserves.

In a new effort to widen the Kingdom's industrial base, Abdul Aziz Al-Zamil, the Minister for Industry and Electricity, announced in January, 1984, that a newly established National Industrialization Company (NIC) will seek overseas joint venture partners to participate in plans for the local manufacture of a variety of goods. The NIC also will seek partners to support its plans to boost the country's skills in industrial management, marketing, technology, and maintenance.[7]

Saudi Arabia has embarked upon a massive development program with long-term objectives to diversify the economy and build a strong private sector. Three development plans have been designed that provide a framework to help accomplish these objectives. The First Development Plan (1970-1975) changed the system of determining oil prices and the degree of Saudi Arabia's control over its oil resources. The Second Development Plan (1975-1980) provided stimulus to private enterprise to assist in the implementation of development programs. The Third Development Plan (currently being implemented) has given special priortiy to investment in the producing sectors of agriculture, industry and mining. Government investment-oriented policies have played a great role in diffusing benefits of rapid growth to all sectors of the economy and all parts of the population.

Throughout the past ten years, Saudi Arabia has enjoyed the benefits of steady, careful planning as the country lays a

[7]U.S.-Arab Commerce, (New York: U.S. Arab Chamber of Commerce, March, 1983), p. 7.

strong foundation for continued growth and stability. (See Figure 1.) To continue this growth, Saudi Arabia needs an influx of technical know-how and expertise.

FIGURE 1
Growth in the Private Sector's Share in GDP

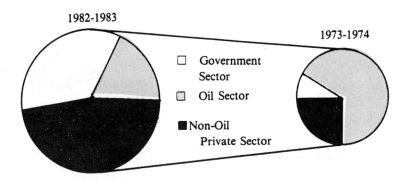

Source: Riyadh, Ministry of Planning, 1984

It is important to note that over the past few years, oil exports have fallen from 9.6 million barrels a day in 1981 to 6.2 million barrels a day in 1982, to an almost certain further decline in 1983 (figures for 1983 are not available). Imports have remained generally stagnant.

As a result of this decline in exports, revenues have also decreased. This trend can been seen in Figure 2:

FIGURE 2
The Fiscal Trend: Revenue and Spending

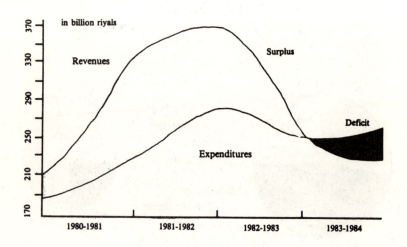

2. What Saudi Arabia Looks Like in the 1980's.

There can be no proper understanding of modernization in Saudi Arabia without an appreciation of certain factors such as religion and oil which have played an important role in Saudi society.

The challenge for the Saudis is to bring their country fully into the twentieth century without sacrificing Arab and Islamic cultural traditions.

Indeed, there is a widespread and fascinating debate taking place in the Islamic countries about the relationship between Islam and modernity. Changes are taking place which cannot easily be reduced to a simple question of whether one should reject Isalm or accept it. It is not that simple, because human societies do not operate in that way. In Saudi Arabia, the real questions are: At what level will religious faith be practiced? Will this faith influence all aspects of life in society, or just some of them?

The Saudi government is determined to achieve modernization without Westernization. If the Saudis succeed in achieving this objective, Saudi Arabia will replace Japan as the modern-day development model, and people will study this model in Saudi universities.

Japan has modernized with spectacular success, yet it has been able to preserve many traditional Japanese ways. The Chinese are also in the process of modernization. They, too, seem able to maintain a compromise between modern values and behavior and traditional culture.

Japan began to acquire European production methods in the nineteenth century, but the Japanese retained their traditional consumption habits. In contrast, the people of the Middle East learned to consume first and only recently began to adopt Western production methods.

Every country has at least three national purposes; national survival, material well-being, and national prestige, usually in that order of priority. Some countries, like the United States, have a fourth national purpose; to promote the quality of life of the individual citizen (life, liberty and the pursuit of happiness).

Saudi Arabia is one of the few countries in the world

explicitly dedicated to promoting a particular religion and a particular religious way of life as the means of happiness to every individual citizen. It is probably the only country in which a specific concept of spiritual well-being is truly the highest national purpose, in fact as well as in rhetoric.[8]

The Hanbal school of Islamic law, which prevails in Saudi Arabia, provides that nothing has any meaning in human affairs except as an expression of divine will. The meaning of all things is to be found only in theology, which expalins the nature of God, and in the Shari'ah, which applies his will to human action.

The Saudi leaders recognize the need to modernize in order to survive as an independent country. A rapidly changing world forces the Saudis to prepare for a number of challenges inherent in the modernization process. Saudis are convinced that they have the tools to meet these challenges successfully.

Modernization depends on a broad set of internal conditions within developing societies. It is also dependent upon external conditions, and the degree to which the international system fosters dependency or competition. There are four phases of modernization; 1) urbanization, 2) literacy, 3) media participation, and 4) political participation.

It is necessary to know and understand the economic conditions and trends of the past in order to gain perspective on contemporary and future directions of modernization in Saudi Arabia.

A widespread misconception about Saudi Arabia is that the country is not a modern nation-state, but rather, a less

---

[8]Robert D. Crane, *Planning the Future of Saudi Arabia: A Model for Achieving National Priorities,* (New York: Praeger, 1978), p. 37.

developed federation of tribes, led by religious leaders and the Royal Family.

It is true that in the late 1930's there was little more in Saudi Arabia than Bedouins, camels, and sand. At that time, there were no roads, no automobiles, few villages, and no trees. There was open desert everywhere. Cities such as as Riyadh and Jeddah were very small, with few streets suitable for automobiles. People rode camels as prevalently as we ride in automobiles today.

Prior to the discovery of oil, very few Arabs in Saudi Arabia had any education, and those who did came mostly from the Red Sea coastal area where they had more contact with the outside world. The merchants from this area and, in particular, their sons, often went to Cairo for their elementary school education.

In contrast, Saudi Arabia is now as modern a place as other developed countries. Some examples of the country's progress are indicated below:

— King Khalid International Airport, in Riyadh (the Royal Capital of Saudi Arabia), is one of the largest and most expensive in the world.

— The new city of Madinat Al-Jubail Al-Siniyah (Jubail) will hold a community of nearly 400,000 people; it has oil refineries and manufacturing facilities for petroleum chemicals, fertilizer, aluminum, steel, and other products in a vast industrial park that provides almost every major requirement of a thriving and developing nation. The section of Jubail under development is linked to Yanbu, its sister city in the West. Yanbu is being shaped into one of the world's most impressive industrial complexes.

Within a few years, Madinat Yanbu Al-Siniyah will become one of the biggest cities in the Kingdom, with an independent port for each of the following types of exports; industrial, oil, crude, natural gas, and commercial.[9] (See Appendix 12).

— Free medical and hospital services are available to everyone. The number of hospitals and clinics is being increased, and public health has improved. Increasing urbanization has been accompanied by improvements in housing. New hotels and restaurants, along with a wealth of consumer goods, are all part of modern Saudi Arabia.

— Industrial projects for the production of fertilizers, steel, petrochemicals, cement, glass, and plastics are being rapidly developed to lessen Saudi Arabia's dependence on crude oil exports. (See Appendix 14).

Needed infrastructure has been built, including highways, pipelines, ports, airports, and industrial complexes such as Yanbu and Jubail. Today, there are over 15,000 miles of paved roads—before 1950 there were virtually none—with 1,100 miles of new roads being built each year. Some of the world's largest seawater desalination plants provide drinking water. Advanced automatic telephone systems, television, and radio are in operation in all major cities, towns, and villages.

— Transportation and communication are vital to the development of any growing nation. As part of this growth, SAUDIA, the Kingdom's national airline, has

[9]Dr. Yusuf Ibrahim Al-Turki, Director General of the Royal Commission for Yanbu, explained that once the Royal Commission's project is completed, Madinat Yanbu Al-Siniyah will have a population of 150,000 people.

connected all major cities and most smaller towns throughout Saudi Arabia (See Appendix 8). The camel is no longer the principle form of transportation. Instead it is raised for its meat, wool, and milk.

Also, modern communications systems, including Telex, international telephones, cables, and telegrams, are available.

— Modern water distribution keeps the Kingdom's fields green.

— The Kingdom became the tenth foreign participant in the U.S. Landsat program with an accord signed in Washington by the Saudi Finance Minister. This will allow the Saudi government to receive and distribute data gathered by the U.S. satellite system. Saudi Arabia will build ground receiving stations to process Landsat earth resources data useful for Saudi agricultural and other development projects.

— The number of Saudi students in the U.S. has grown from 58 in 1980 to 10,000 in 1984:

       Engineering, 32.1%

       Business, 17.6%

       Undergraduate students, more than 70%

       Graduate students, 21.1%

       Doctoral or Post-Doctoral students, 7.7%[10]

— See Appendix 7 for information on education in Saudi Arabia.

— Saudi Arabia ranks fourth in the world production of dates. The Kingdom's Eastern province, with over two million date palm trees, produces a surplus of the fruit, which it now exports to neighboring Gulf countries.

[10] Embassy of Saudi Arabia, Information Office, Washington, D.C., October 15, 1984.

Petromin,[11] SABIC (the Saudi Basic Industries Corporation), the Royal Commission for Jubail and Yanbu, and
other similar governmental establishments are entrusted
with implementation of the massive capital projects.

It surprises some people to learn that among the techno-
logical products Saudi Arabia has begun to manufacture (on
a limited basis), are the following:

*Radios, satellite receivers, integrated circuits, semiconductors, resis-
tors, fiber optic cables, VHF transmitters, circuit cards, microchips,
head sets, electronic switching components, mobile radio telephones,
subassemblies, parts and support equipment.*

In this regard, we may draw attention to the significance of American oil companies. These companies have
helped develop Saudi Arabia's natural resources, and have
thus played a key role in influencing modern Saudi
society. (See Appendix 10).

Aramco, for example, is a major force in Middle Eastern
affairs. Aramco is the developer of the Kingdom's energy
resources, and has helped to train many Saudis. Aramco's
work includes massive exploration and drilling efforts,
operation of the world's largest onshore and offshore oil
fields, and huge oil processing operations.[12]

Aramco is also involved in many other projects within

---

[11] The first national company in the Kingdom, its significant contribution to the
economy of Saudi Arabia cannot be overstated, due to its emphasis on
"Saudization" of the company by means of training and hiring native Saudis
rather than nationals of foreign countries.

[12] Aramco has been operating successfully in Saudi Arabia since 1933. Over this
half century, Aramco has developed into the world's largest crude oil and
natural gas liquids producing company.

the Kingdom, both directly and indirectly related to energy production. These include:

— The operation of a mammoth seawater treatment plant to provide the millions of barrels of non-potable water needed each day for injection into oil fields for reservoir pressure support.
— Managing a global communication network which serves Aramco's worldwide operations.
— Expanding and maintaining the elaborate electronic data processing systems that are so essential to the company's operations.
— Planning, designing, and constructing complete industrial complexes, as well as residential communities, for Aramco's employees.

Of the many business ties between the United States and Saudi Arabia, the United States-Saudi Arabian Joint Commission on Economic Cooperation is easily one of the most significant. This government-to-government program has undertaken a variety of projects in various economic sectors. There are nineteen major projects involving eleven Saudi Arabian government ministries and eleven U.S. government departments and agencies.

The Saudi government realizes that oil is a limited resource, and this has led them to seek ways to transfer oil resources into "real wealth."[13]

---

[13]We must stress that development occurs when misallocations are eliminated. The economy "grows" as resources are shifted toward their more highly valued uses. This is a temporary source of "growth," but it may have dynamic implications. However, the Kingdom guarantees free enterprise provided that it does not conflict with the public interest.

This goal has evolved into the development of an industrial economy to provide production work for the citizens of Saudi Arabia. This has been done with the aid of formal economic planning, divided into a series of five-year plans which are implemented by the Planning Ministry.

The Planning Ministry is vital to the development of Saudi Arabia. The Ministry has played a key role in determining national priorities, devising development plans, coordinating the public and private sectors and the various levels of government, and providing and monitoring implementation to insure that the goal of development will be achieved.

The basic aims of these policy measures are increased Saudi participation in the development of the economy, expansion of the private sector, and achievement of a number of social objectives.[14]

It is important to highlight the overall achievement of the First and Second Development Plans (1970-1980). These accomplishments can be summarized as follows:[15]

— Rural-urban migration within the country has been extensive, including many nomadic Bedouins who have settled on the outskirts of the cities.
— Actual state expenditures rose from Saudi Riyal six billion to SR 186 billion, an astronomical increase.
— Actual development project expenditures rose by an annual rate of 54 percent.
— The Gross Domestic Production (GDP) grew at an

[14]Planning Ministry, planning books on the Second and Third Development Plans, Riyadh, Saudi Arabia. Execution of Saudi Arabia's Five-Year Plan, covering the period from 1980 through 1985, began in mid-May, 1980.
[15]Arab News, Jeddah, August 23, 1982.

annual average rate of 10.7 percent during the decade, from SR 17 billion to SR 49 billion.

— The agricultural sector attained an average growth rate of 5.3 percent, while its share of the GDP fell from 13 to 6.5 percent.

— Crude oil and natural gas sectors had an annual growth rate of 9.1 percent, increasing participation in the GDP from 84.7 percent to 91.6 percent.

— The petroleum refining sector had a 3.2 percent annual growth rate, although its contribution to the GDP dropped from 13 percent to 7.6 percent.

— Due to the accelerated economic development in this ten-year period, the share of contributions for machinery and transport in the real gross fixed capital formation increased from 24 percent to 45.3 percent. At the same time, the participation of the construction sector decreased from 75.8 percent to 54.7 percent. However, foreign trade has increased during the last decade (see Table 5).

— The average growth rate in petroleum production was 20 percent until 1973, when its value increased from SR 9.6 billion to SR 20 billion.

— The production growth of the non-petroleum sector increased at an annual rate of 13 percent.

— Saudi Arabia has become one of the richest countries in the world in terms of per capita income.

To sum up, Saudi Arabia's oil sector dominates the economy in terms of: 1) Gross Domestic Product, 2) government revenues, and 3) exports. Due to modifications in the infrastructure and industrial base, there will be an increasing export of refined petroleum products. Crude oil exports will vary. The overall impact of changes in exports will depend on: 1) resulting changes in technology, 2) the propensity to import, 3) the extent to which investment opportunities are generated, 4) the ability to attract foreign investment, and 5) other non-quantitative effects.

It is important to point out that the structure of non-oil sectors is based upon three major flows: 1) The flow of produced and imported goods into the inventory, 2) the flow of orders to the sector, and 3) the flow of shipments to the various demanders.

It is clear, however, that Saudi Arabia's oil revenues have created numerous incentives for the non-oil sector, and that sector has generated spread and linkage effects throughout the economy.

The principle characteristics of Saudi Arabia's development are not simply a consequence of the petroleum industry. Rather, they result from the economic policies pursued by the government in an environment heavily influenced by the existence of the petroleum industry. Moreover, the current and future role of the petroleum industry in Saudi modernization is in large measure a consequence of government policies and sociocultural conditions.

The Saudi economy has grown more rapidly in the past two decades than that of many other nations. In 1982/1983, the Gross Domestic Product (GDP) reached about SR 410 billion (approximately $120 billion), representing a real growth rate (non-oil GDP) of 7.5 percent. The GDP is estimated at 6.5 percent for fiscal 1983-1984.

The liberal economic philosophy of the Kingdom has contributed significantly to this marked economic growth.[16]

[16] No segment of the society has been left untouched and no one can yet know the full extent of the social changes.

By virtue of its success, the liberal economy of the Kingdom of Saudi Arabia can be considered an instructive model. It has its origins in the very nature of the Saudis. Its economic philosophy is inspired by the revelation of the true Islamic religion, which calls for the practice of free trade under conditions of honorable competition, free from the exclusive power of the state, whatever the form of economic activity.

Social services, such as health care, education, and manpower training, continue to be high priorities and will also be emphasized in the upcoming 1985-1990 Development Plan.

TABLE 5
SAUDI ARABIA'S FOREIGN TRADE
(1970-1980) (SR. MILLION)

Hijri	Gregorian	Exports	Percent Changes	Imports	Percent Changes
1389-90	1970	10,907.2	14.9	3,196.8	-5.3
1390-91	1971	17,302.7	58.6	4,708.3	28.4
1391-92	1972	22,761.2	31.6	4,708.3	28.4
1392-93	1973	33,309.1	46.3	7,310.2	55.3
1393-94	1974	126,222.9	278.9	10,149.2	38.8
1394-95	1975	104,411.7	-17.3	14,823.0	46.1
1395-96	1976	135,153.5	29.4	30,691.0	107.0
1396-97	1977	153,208.6	13.4	51,662.0	68.3
1397-98	1978	138,242.0	-9.8	69,179.7	33.9
1398-99	1979	213,183.4	54.2	82,223.3	18.9
1399-1400	1980	362,885.7	70.2	100,349.6	22.1

Source: Annual Report, Saudi Arabian Monetary Agency (SAMA) (Riyadh, Saudi Arabia, 1981), p. 148.

The reader will note the extremely high percentage of exports in 1974. This is due to the significant increase following the oil embargo of 1973.

CONCLUSION

Few countries have experienced a faster pace of social and economic change than Saudi Arabia has in the last decade. The development of oil industries has uniquely altered the fabric of life in Saudi Arabia. Until the middle of this century, Saudi Arabia was one of the world's poorest countries. Today, the Kingdom has one of the highest per capita incomes.

There is much to be gained, and many misconceptions can be avoided, if we understand the modernization philosophy of Saudi Arabia. Central to this philosophy is the reliance upon and preservation of Islamic values. In addition, Saudi leaders are careful to differentiate between modernization and development. Development is a comprehensive process, whereas modernization can be seen as the material aspect of development.

Saudi leaders understand the psychological, social, cultural, political, and economic dimensions of development. They emphasize human as well as economic developments, which work together to achieve national development.

The Islamic state serves to promote the spiritual and material aspects of life which form the foundations of true human well-being and happiness. The centerpiece of Islamic public finance and fiscal policy is *zakat*, the tax on wealth designed to benefit the poor and discourage hoarding.[17]

[17]Efforts to maximize wealth, hoarding, profiting at the expense of others, surplus earnings, and gambling are all considered immoral. Insurance is outlawed in Saudi Arabia as a form of gambling.

The Saudis reject capitalism due to its exploitation of labor, its speculative market and interest rates, and its failure to maintain full employment and insure free competition. Socialism and communism are rejected due to the nature of the moral and spiritual development they promote, their lack of freedom of choice and action, their restrictions on private property and free enterprise, and their exploitation of man by the state. Islam, on the other hand, is said to transcend these systems by making the individual a servant of God and society. This general orientation leads to basic agreement on the principles of development in Saudi Arabia.

Many Saudis sincerely feel that their sudden prosperity is due to their devotion to Islam, including their adherence to its stricter tenets. They see their well-being as a manifestation of their faith. This is expressed in the words, *Allah Kareem,* which means, "God is generous."

Oil, as we know, continues to be essential to the development and modernization of Saudi Arabia. Islam, however, as both a religion and a system of government (*diin wa dawlah*), will remain a powerful and popular force in Saudi Arabia. It will continue to be an important factor in the modernization process, minimizing Westernization, and helping to create a unique and successful model of development.

PART FOUR

APPENDIX 1

Saudi Leadership

*King Fahd,
Born 1922, took office
in June, 1982.*

Under the inspiration and leadership of King Fahd (top), Prince Abdullah bin Abdul Aziz, Crown Prince, Deputy Prime Minister and Head of the National Guard (right), and H.R.H. Prince Sultan Ibn Abdul Aziz, Minister of Defense and Aviation, Inspector General, and Second Deputy Premier (left), the Kingdom has managed to temper progress with loyalty to Islamic principles and Saudi culture.

APPENDIX 2

The Flag of the Kingdom of Saudi Arabia

The Saudi Flag is inscribed with the creed; "There is no god but Allah, Muhammad is the Messenger of God." Below it, there is an Arabian curved sword with its hilt directed towards the mast. The sword and the lettering are white, and the background is green.

APPENDIX 3

The opening words of the Qur'an are, "In the name of Allah, The Compassionate, The Merciful." This phrase is printed across the top of every sheet of official paper in Saudi Arabia, and on all personal correspondence.

Muslims are supposed to begin all acts with the name of Allah, with the word "Basmallah."

For example, the pilots of Saudia (Saudi Airlines) welcome all passengers on each flight by first saying, "Basmallah."

The picture above is the official symbol of Saudi Arabia.

The swords, always unsheathed, symbolize strength rooted in faith.

The date palm, which traditionally supplied the main agricultural crop, is emblematic of vitality and growth.

APPENDIX 4

The Five Pillars of Islam

1. The profession of faith (*Shahada*)*

2. Prayer (*Al-Salat*)

3. Payment of taxes (*Zakat*)

4. Fast (*Al-Sawm*)

5. The Pilgrimage (*Hajj*)

*The individual simply repeats, in Arabic, "There is no god but Allah, and Muhammad is his Messenger." The *shahadah* is the first major requirement for becoming a Muslim.

APPENDIX 5

The Hajj

The Pilgrimage to Makkah

It is no exaggeration to say that the Hajj, to the average Muslim, is the climax of his temporal existence. It is a form of spiritual fulfillment which he shares and celebrates with the entire world of Islam.

The Hajj—the pilgrimage to Makkah—is essentially a series of rites performed in and near Makkah, the holiest of the three holy cities of Islam—Makkah, Medina, and Jerusalem.

The trip to Medina carries the pilgrims through the early heroic years of Islam. It starts as soon as they turn inland from the Red Sea and approach the small village of Badr, where the Muslims, then a numerically weak religious sect, fought and won the battle that eventually sent them westward to North Africa and Spain and eastward to India.

As one of the Five Pillars of Islam—that is, one of the five basic requirements for Muslims—all believers, if they can afford it and are healthy enough, must make pilgrimage at least once in their lives. Significantly, the annual pilgrimage to Makkah presents one of the biggest people-moving challenges in the world. The Hajj places a special burden on the government of Saudi Arabia to insure that the millions of pilgrims can be accommodated and worship.

APPENDIX 6

Former Rulers of the Kingdom

1. **H.M. The late King Abdul Aziz Ibn Abdul Rahman Al Saud**
Abdul Aziz "Ibn Saud"
Born 1876
Ruled 1902-1953
Died 1953

Ibn Saud, the founder of Saudi Arabia, was the "Imam" of his people as well as the King.

2. **Saud, son of Abdul Aziz**
Born 1902
Ruled 1953-1964
Died 1969

3. **Faisal, son of Abdul Aziz**
Born 1904
Ruled from 1964 until his assassination in 1975

Under the remarkable leadership of the late King Faisal, the Kingdom rose to a position of authority in the world.

4. **Khalid, son of Abdul Aziz**
Born 1912
Ruled 1975-1982
Died 1982

The late King Khalid was a devout man, traditional and honest.

APPENDIX 7

Education

Education is a primary factor in any development program. It must be emphasized that since the establishment of the Kingdom of Saudi Arabia, education has become one of the fastest-growing areas of social development.

The improvement in the country's education has contributed greatly to the development of the country as a whole. As a result of growing higher education enrollments, the number of universities has increased to seven, distributed among the Kingdom's provinces. They are; King Saud University, Imam Muhammad Ibn Saud Islamic University (in Riyadh), King Abdul Aziz University (in Jeddah), the Isamic University (in Medina), Um-Al-Qora University (in Makkah), the University of Petroleum and Minerals (in Dhahran), and King Faisal University (in Al-Ahsa). There are extension campuses of these seven universities, giving a total of sixteen university and college campuses throughout the country. These include colleges of education for women, teachers' institutes, and vocational and technical institutes.

Every year many postgraduate students are sent abroad by the Ministry of Higher Education and other governmental bodies to pursue advanced specialized studies at the most highly reputed universities in the world. All education is free, and students may progress as rapidly as their abilities allow; they may also study abroad at the government's expense.* This is necessary in order for them to be able to manage the country's developing facilities.

*Over 10,000 Saudi Arabian students are studying in the United States.

APPENDIX 8

Saudia

SAUDIA, the Kingdom's national air carrier, has taken a leading place among airlines in the Middle East.

This can be realized when we consider its large fleet of aircraft, the number of passengers, its highly sophisticated equipment, and the services rendered to its passengers.

Saudi Arabian Airlines carries most of the long distance passenger traffic between the Kingdom and the main cities of the Middle East, Asia, Africa, Europe, and the United States.

No alcohol is served on the plane; you may choose from Western or Middle Eastern food, but no ham or pork will be available. On domestic flights, dates and a special Saudi coffee are served. The flight attendant greets the passengers in the name of Allah.

A traveler using any of Saudi Arabia's large international airports can expect to be on time at least nine times out of ten.

APPENDIX 9

Major autonomous agencies in Saudi Arabia.

- Royal Commission for Jubail and Yanbu
- Saudi Arabian Airlines
- Saudi Arabian Center for Science and Technology
- Saudi Industrial Development
- Saudi Fund for Development
- Saudi Basic Industries Corporation
- Saudi Consulting House
- Directorate General of Zakat and Income Tax
- General Organization for Social Insurance
- General Ports Authority
- Customs Department
- Agriculture Research Center
- International Airport Projects
- Grain Silos and Flour
- King Faisal Foundation
- Petromin
- Saline Water Conversion
- Saudi Arabian Monetary Agency
- Saudi Arabian Standards Organization
- Youth Welfare Organization
- Saudi Government Railroad Organization
- Saudi Arabian Agricultural Bank

- Central Department of Statistics
  (Ministry of Finance and National Economy)
- Directorate General for Mineral Resources
- Jeddah Seaport
- Dammam Seaport
- General Secretariat for Arab Red Crescent and
  Red Cross
- Presidency of Civil Aviation
- Government Electricity Organization
- Meteorology and Environmental Protection Agency

Source: Ministry of Commerce, Riyadh, Saudi Arabia (1984)

APPENDIX 10

U.S. Firms in the Kingdom

The following companies, listed alphabetically, have made significant contributions to the economic development of Saudi Arabia.

Aramco Services
Arthur Young & Company
Avco Corporation
Bechtel (See Appendix 11)
The BDM Corporation
The Bendix Corporation
Booz-Allen & Hamilton
Brown & Root, Inc.
Burrough Corporation
C.A.C.I., Inc.
Camp Dresser & McKee
Comset Corporation
Chrysler Corporation
Computer Sciences Corporation
Catalytic, Inc.
DMJM Corporation
Dresser Industries, Inc.
Dynalectron
EG & G
Exxon Corporation

Frank E. Basil, Inc.
Foster Wheeler Energy Corporation
Fluor Engineers and Constructors
General Motors Corporation
General Electric Corporation
HBH Company
Holmes & Nerver
Honeywell
Hughes Aircraft Company
Hospital Corporation of America
John Deere
Litton
Lockheed
M.W. Kellog Company
McDonnell Douglas Corporation
Mobil Oil Company
National Medical Enterprises
Northrup Corporation
Page Tech. Services, Inc.
Planning Research Corporation
Proctor & Gamble Company
RCA Corporation
The Ralph M. Parsons Company
Science Applications International, Inc.
Shell Oil
Sperry International
Standard Oil of California

Teledyne, Inc.

Tracor

Texas Instruments

Union Carbide Company

Vinnell Corporation

Vulcan Materials Company

Watermark Systems, Inc.

Western Electric Company

Westinghouse Company*

Whittaker International Services

*Westinghouse serves the Kingdom's growing markets in energy, construction, transportation, defense, and industry services.

APPENDIX 11

BECHTEL

It was the maturing of the petroleum age that first drew Bechtel overseas, and it is in the Middle East that some of the world's most significant deposits of oil have been found. Bechtel has had forty years of industrial growth in the Kingdom of Saudi Arabia, due to its significant contribution to the country. Examples of Bechtel's contributions to modernization of Saudi Arabia include:

— Madinat Al-Jubail Al-Siniyah, one of the most ambitious civil engineering and construction endeavors of the twentieth century.

— Engineering and construction of port facilities at the Gulf Coast city of Dammam, construction work of the Riyadh-to-Dammam railroad, road repair and maintenance, communications systems, production facilities at the Abqaiq, Ain Dar, and Shedhum oil fields; water desalination facilities and Ghazlan power plant; continued work at the Ras Tanura refinery.

— Providing engineering, procurement and construction management services for the development of a petrochemical processing plant of Yanbu.

— King Khalid International Airport (KKIA) in the Royal Capital of Saudi Arabia is one of the largest and most expensive in the world. The airport will be capable of handling twenty million passengers annually by the year 2000. Bechtel is also working on another new airport near the Arabian Gulf Coast city of Dammam.

Former Bechtel executive George Shultz, the U.S. Secretary of State, believes that, "Bechtel is a truly remarkable organization, astonishing in the range of its capabilities, and impressive in the quality of its people, who bring integrity, intelligence, enthusiasm and drive to their work."*

*Interestingly, Shultz's statement was made at the time of his confirmation as Secretary of State by the U.S. Senate on July 15, 1982.

APPENDIX 12

Madinat Yanbu Al-Siniyah

A new city rises from the sands of Arabia. By the year 2006, the new city will be one of the world's largest and most sophisticated energy centers. The city will help Saudi Arabia achieve some of its major national goals, including its primary one; the diversification of its crude oil-based economy.

The starting point for the industrialization project in the western province was the selection, in 1976, of Parsons, to develop a thirty-year master plan for Yanbu.

Today, the industrial city of Yanbu is taking shape. The crude oil terminal is in place, and the port is in operation. Some of the largest supertankers in the world are loading oil at Yanbu, then sailing for refineries around the world.

One of the world's largest barge-mounted water desalination plants is providing fresh water. Electrical power is available, and thousands of telephone lines are operational.

One of the most sophisticated telecommunications networks on earth will be in place in Yanbu by 1985.

For the better part of three decades, an important role in the growth and development of the Middle East has been played by the Parsons group of companies, including the Ralph M. Parsons Company, DeLeuw, Cather & Co, S.I.P. Engineering, Inc., and Engineering-Science, Inc.

The new city is characterized by the best of modern conveniences, with interior and exterior features congenial to Saudi Arabian traditional lifestyle. It is a modern city which reflects the distinctive tradition of Saudi Arbian culture.

APPENDIX 13

Prominent Saudi Firms

- Abdul Aziz and Mohammad Abdullah Al Jomaith
- Abalkhail Consulting Engineers
- Abdullah Said Bughsan & Brothers
- A.A. Truki Corporation
- ALIRIZA Company
- Abdul Aziz Zaidan & Partners
- Al Jafali & Partners
- Abdul Latif Jamil Company
- Al Zamil Company
- Al Gossaibi Company
- Dallah AVCO
- KAKI
- Olayan Company
- Tamimi & Fouad (TAFCO)
- National Pipe Company
- REDEC
- Al Akeel Company
- Al Rajehi Establishment
- General Arabian Medical & Allied Services Ltd., (GAMA)
- NABCO
- Al-Ajou
- Ben Ladin Company

- Saudi International Rice Company
- Mansour Company
- Al Qahtani Trading Company
- Arabian Business & Management
- SIYANCO
- Dar Alwatan
- Al-Bawardy Consulting Engineers
- Arabian Development Company
- Omar A. Balubaid Establishment
- Saudi Arabian Trading & Construction Company
- El Khereiji Company
- Al Rashid Company
- Al Khodairi Company

APPENDIX 14

Saudi Petrochemical Company (SADAF)*

The company was formed as a joint venture between the Saudi Basic Industries Corporation (SABIC) and Pecton Arabian Limited, an affiliate of Shell Oil Company, U.S.A. Sadaf builds a foundation for the future. The venture is part of the industrialization of Saudi Arabia and will provide a long-term supply of basic petrochemicals to local and world markets. The company will transform ethane, benzene and salt brine into ethylene, styrene, crude industrial ethanol, ethylene dichloride, and caustic soda. These products will be marketed in Saudi Arabia and throughout the world. Because the uses of Sadaf's products are so widespread, all of Sadaf's products will find receptive domestic and international markets. Furthermore, training and development of all Saudi nationals receives considerable attention from the Board and management of the company.

*In November 1980, the company was officially registered as a Saudi Co. The company adopted the Arabic name, Sadaf, which means "seashells." A most appropriate name considering both the past history of the town of Jubail and the ready identification of the shell as a symbol of the one partner.

SELECTED
BIBLIOGRAPHY

SELECTED BIBLIOGRAPHY

Books

Al-Farsy, Fouad. *Saudi Arabia: A Case Study in Development.* London: Stacey International, 1980.

Alkuhuli, Mohammadi Ali. *The Light of Islam.* Saudi Arabia 1981.

Al-Omar, Abdul-Rahman Bin Hamad. *Islam: The Religion of Truth.* Riyadh: Farazdak Press, 1395H

Awan, Akhtar A. *Equality, Efficiency and Property Ownership in the Islamic Economic System.* Lanham, Md.: University Press of America, 1983.

Biersted, Robert. *The Social Order.* New York: McGraw Hill, 1974.

Boisard, Marcel A. *L'Islam et la Morale Internationale.* Paris: A. Michel, 1979.

Bottomore, T.B. *Sociology: A Guide to Problems and Literature.* New York: Random House, Vintage Book, 1972.

Bozdag, Ismet. *The Third Idea the World is Waiting For: Socio-economic Model of Islam.* Karachi: National Book Foundation, 1979.

Brown, Lester. *World Without Borders.* New York: Vintage Books, 1973.

Burr, J., ed. *Handbook of Developments in World Philosophy.* Westport, Conn., 1980.

Coelho, George V., and Paul I. Ahmed *Uprooting and Development: Dilemmas of Coping with Modernization.* New York, Plenum Press, 1980.

Cottrell, Alvin J. *The Persian Gulf.* Baltimore: The Johns Hopkins University Press, 1980.

Curtis, Michael, ed. *Religion and Politics in the Middle East.* Boulder: Westview Press, 1981.

Donohue, John J. and John L. Esposito. *Islam in Transition: Muslim Perspective.* New York: Oxford University Press, 1982.

Downs, James F. *Cultures in Crisis.* Beverly Hills, CA: Glencoe Press, 1971.

El-Daghistani. "The Evolution of the Moslem Family in the Middle East Countries." *Readings in Arab Middle East Societies and Cultures,* Paris: Mouton, 1970.

El Maliakh, Ragaei. *Saudi Arabia, Rush to Development.* London: Croom Helm, 1982.

El Mallakh, Ragaie, and Dorothea H. El Mallakh, eds. *Saudi Arabia: Energy, Developmental Planning, and Industrialization.* Lexington, Mass.: Lexington Books, 1982.

Enayat, Hamid. *Modern Islamic Political Thought.* Austin: University of Texas Press, 1982.

Esposito, John L. *Islam and Development: Religion & Sociopolitical Change.* Syracuse, New York: New York University Press, 1980.

Firt, R., quoted by T.B. Bottomore, in *Sociology: A Guide to Problems and Literature.* New York: Random House, 1972.

Global Justice and Development: Report of the Aspen Inter-Religious Consultation, June, 1974. Washington, D.C.: Overseas Development Council, 1974.

Goode, William J. *World Revolution and Family Patterns.* New York: The Free Press, 1963.

Gouldner, Alvin W. *The Future of Intellectuals and The Rise of the New Class.* Oxford: Oxford University Press, 1982.

Goulet, Denis. *A New Moral Order: Development Ethics and Liberation Theology.* Maryknoll, New York: Orbis Books, 1974.

Halliday, Fred. *Arabia Without Sultans: A Political Survey of Instability in the Arab World.* New York: Vintage Books, 1975.

Hanafi, Hasan. *Matha Yaani al-Yasar al-Islami (What is the Meaning of the Islamic Left), Vol. 1,* Cairo: January 1981.

Harman, Willis W. *An Incomplete Guide to the Future.* New York: W.W. Norton and Company., 1979.

Harris, Marvin. *The Rise of Anthropological Theory.* New York: Harper and Row Co., 1968.

Hassan, Farooq. *The Concept of State and Law in Islam.* Washington, D.C.: University Press of America, 1981.

Hodgson, Marshall G. *The Venture of Islam: Conscience and History in a World Civilization.* Chicago: University of Chicago Press, 1974.

Islami, A. Reza S. *The Political Economy of Saudi Arabia and the Arab Gulf States.* New York: Inter-Crescent Publishing and Information Corporation, 1979.

Lackner, Helen. *A House Built on Sand: A Political Economy of Saudi Arabia.* London: Ithaca Press, 1978.

Levitas, Gloria B. *Culture and Consciousness.* New York: George Braziller, Inc., 1967.

Looney, Robert. *Saudi Arabia's Development Potential.* Lexington, Mass.: Lexington Books, 1982.

Mansfield, Peter. *The New Arabians.* Chicago: J.C. Ferguson Publishing Co., 1981.

Moliver, Donald M., and Paul J. Abbondante. *The Economy of Saudi Arabia.* New York: Praeger, 1980.

Muslehuddim, Mohammad. *Sociology and Islam: A Comparative Study of Islam and its Social System.* Lahore: Islamic Publications Limited, 1977.

The Muslim World and The Future Economic Order: Report of the Islamic Council of Europe. London: ICE, 1979.

Niblock, Tim, ed. *Social and Economic Development in the Arab Gulf.* London: Croom Helm, 1980.

Patai, Ralph. *The Arab Mind.* New York: Charles Schribner's Sons, 1973.

Shaw, John A., and David E. Long. *Saudi Arabian Modernization.* New York: Praeger, 1982.

Stookey, Robert W. *The Arabian Peninsula: Zone of Ferment.* Stanford, CA: Hoover Institution Press, 1984.

Shilling, Nancy A. *Doing Business in Saudi Arbia and the Arab Gulf States.* New York: Inter-Crescent Publishing and Information Corporation, 1979.

Smith, Wilfred C. *Islam in Modern History.* Princeton, New Jersey: Princeton University Press, 1977.

Quandt, William B. *Saudi Arabia in the 1980's: Foreign Policy and Oil.* Washington, D.C.: The Brookings Institution, 1981.

Said, Edward, and Faud Sulieman. *The Arab Today: Alternative for Tomorrow.* Columbus, Ohio: Forum Associates, Inc. 1973.

Wells, Donald A. *Saudi Arabian Development Strategy.* Washington, D.C.: American Enterprise Institute for Public Policy Research, 1976.

Periodicals

Arab News, Jeddah, Saudi Arabia, August 23, 1982.

Christian Science Monitor, May 9, 1984.

Davilov, S. "The Arab Muslim Image of World Order," *Middle East Review,* Vol. 11, No. 4, 1979.

Enayat, Hamid. "The Resurgence of Islam I: The Background," *History Today,* February, 1980.

Hodgson, Marshall G.S. "The Role of Islam in World History" *International Journal of Middle East Studies,* Vol. 1, 1970.

Jameson, Kenneth P. and Charles K. Wilber, eds. "Religious Values and Development," *World Development,* Vol. 8, No. 7/8, July/August, 1980.

Kagaya, Kan. "Islam as a Modern Social Force," *The Developing Economies,* Vol. IV, No. 1, 1960.

Lewis, Bernard. "The Return of Islam" *Commentary,* Jan. 1976.

Liebesny, Herbert J. "Judicial Systems in the Near and Middle East: Evolutionary Development and Islamic Revival" *The Middle East Journal,* Vol. 37, No. 2, Spring 1983.

Nyang, Sulayman S. "The Islamic State and Economic Development: A Theoretical Analysis" *Islamic Culture,* Vol. 50, No. 1, January, 1976.

Ruthven, Malise. "Sunni Islam: The Well-Beaten Path," *The Events,* January 13, 1978.

Said, Abdul Aziz. "Precepts and Practice of Human Rights in Islam," *Univ. Human Rights Journal* Vol. 1, No. 1, January-March, 1979.

Saudi Arabia, Saudi Arabian Information Office, Washington, D.C.: Vol. 1, No. 1, Spring, 1984.

Saudi Arabian Monetary Agency, The Government Printer, Saudi Arabia, 1981.

Time, "The World of Islam," April 16, 1979.

U.S. Arab Commerce, New York, March, 1984.